One Semester Away from a Crisis

One Semester Away from a Crisis

An Economist's Perspective on Leading Small Colleges

WILLIAM T. BOGART

Rutgers University Press
New Brunswick, Camden, and Newark, New Jersey
London

Rutgers University Press is a department of Rutgers, The State University of New Jersey, one of the leading public research universities in the nation. By publishing worldwide, it furthers the University's mission of dedication to excellence in teaching, scholarship, research, and clinical care.

A British Cataloging-in-Publication record for this book is available from the British Library.

978-1-9788-4530-5 (cloth)
978-1-9788-4529-9 (paper)
978-1-9788-4531-2 (epub)

Cataloging-in-publication data is available from the Library of Congress.
LCCN 2025030597

∞ The paper used in this publication meets the requirements of the American National Standard for Information Sciences—Permanence of Paper for Printed Library Materials, ANSI Z39.48-1992.

rutgersuniversitypress.org

For Mary

Contents

Prologue

Becoming a President

I didn't intend to become a college president. In fact, I didn't plan on a career in academia. My dad worked for big companies—NASA, Martin-Marietta, IBM—and I grew up around other people whose parents worked for big companies. I figured I'd go to college and then work for a big company.

By choosing to attend Rice University, I had unknowingly chosen to put myself into a rare research environment that prioritized undergraduate teaching. By continuing to graduate school at Princeton University, I unintentionally reinforced that subliminal message. Research universities, in general, are not opposed to excellent undergraduate teaching. It's just not typically a high priority, but Rice and Princeton are exceptions.

Looking back, it was while in graduate school that the idea of being a college president first occurred. Professor Harvey Rosen was leading a discussion in his public finance class on a lovely afternoon in spring 1987. Princeton had just announced that (economist) Harold Shapiro would be the new president to replace retiring president (and economist) William Bowen. Harvey observed, "The first 16 presidents of Princeton were Presbyterian ministers or the sons of Presbyterian ministers, and the last two studied econometrics under Richard Quandt." Naturally, we laughed, because Professor

Quandt was still teaching econometrics, and I was even working for him doing some programming. As I recall, Harvey went on to speculate on what economic concepts would be useful for higher education leadership, with opportunity cost (nothing is free, so every decision involves giving up something) and time value of money (a dollar today is worth more than a dollar tomorrow) being the top two. From the vantage point of today, I can say that those are indeed useful concepts, and in the rest of the book I'll introduce quite a few others.

After completing my PhD, I joined the Weatherhead School of Management at Case Western Reserve University. It was a school of management instead of a business school because of a strong belief that there were common principles in leading for-profit, nonprofit, and government entities. There was also an intentional ethos of "creating value" that permeated everything we did. It was, in fact, that ethos that was fundamental to my decision to move from the research university environment to the teaching college environment.

For most people outside of academia, there probably isn't that obvious a difference among these institutions. Just to give a sense of how momentous a shift that is, consider the reaction to my winning the highest undergraduate teaching award offered by the university. The Carl F. Wittke Award is given to two professors each year, and the award is presented during the commencement ceremony. It's a big deal. I won it in my fourth year at the university. Because it was a six-year tenure track, I was untenured. It was common knowledge that the Wittke Award was often a response by students because a popular teacher was not being awarded tenure. Multiple people offered muted congratulations mixed with concern and sympathy. (By the way, the other professor who won the award that year was a popular math professor who had not been awarded tenure, so the concern was not without foundation.) That is not the peer reaction to someone winning the top teaching award at a teaching college!

I became a professor because I enjoyed research. Once a professor, I discovered I enjoyed teaching and was good at it. I also discovered I enjoyed being part of efforts to organize and lead activities that created an environment for other people to succeed in research and teaching and began to consider moving into leadership. During a sabbatical year spent visiting the University of Michigan, I had the opportunity to learn from a respected colleague who was associate provost that year and became provost soon thereafter. I took two things away from that year. First, I was interested in institutional leadership but not at a huge place like Michigan. Second, some economic ideas were applicable in this realm.

When I returned from sabbatical, I became department chair, the first step on the leadership ladder. Because that was enjoyable and the department was successful, I was considering the next step. It was clear to me that "moving up" in a research university inevitably entailed spending less time and energy on undergraduate education. Because I truly valued that dimension, I was torn. My wife, as she so often does, crystallized the issue for me. "In ten years, would you rather be president of Baldwin Wallace (a teaching college nearby that she graduated from) or dean of the Weatherhead School?" I immediately answered, "president of Baldwin Wallace," making it clear that I needed to start taking steps in that direction. Within two years of that conversation, I was chief academic officer at York College of Pennsylvania, a teaching college, and launched on a two-decade career in leadership.

On Leadership

To obtain a leadership position at a college, a person has to participate in an interesting selection process. One inevitable question is, "Tell us about your leadership style." I've never quite understood what the point of this question is, because it is more informative to examine how a person has actually behaved and performed throughout their career. But from my first interview over twenty years ago through a variety of leadership experiences and interactions with other leaders, I've had the opportunity to reflect on the topic. For what it's worth, here are a few thoughts.

My usual answer to the interview question is that my leadership style is that of a soccer coach. I recruit the best players, put them in positions that fit their strengths, and help them work together to achieve the goals. This approach has several advantages. First, it's true. Second, it is a good fit for how most colleges want their senior leadership team to work (especially as contrasted with the stereotypical micromanagement associated with football coaches). Third, it draws on my own background as a soccer player, which also serves as a reminder of my personal commitment to a college experience that goes beyond the classroom.

A second, more subtle answer to the question emerged over time. You need to understand that I read all the time and interpret much of my life in the context of books. That is not rare among academics, although I believe it is less common in other lines of work. I hope not to resemble the description in a book by Ian Caldwell and Dustin Thomason (2004, 54), but I suspect I do. "I'd begun to realize that there was an unspoken prejudice among book-learned people, a secret conviction they all seemed to share, that life as we know it is an imperfect vision of reality, and that only art, like a pair of reading glasses, can correct it. The scholars and intellectuals I met at our dinner table always seemed to hold a grudge against the world. They could never quite reconcile themselves to the idea that our lives don't follow the dramatic arc that a good author gives to a great literary character." Anyway, a more direct and less metaphorical description of my approach to leadership is drawn from the character of Cletus Graeme in Gordon Dickson's book (1972), *Tactics of Mistake*. In the book, Graeme is a military genius. His antagonist decides that the way to victory is to capture Graeme to prevent him leading the opposition. Despite succeeding in capturing Graeme, his antagonist nevertheless loses. Graeme explains that he has triumphed as a leader by making himself unnecessary, because he has developed the abilities of other people so that they are able to do what previously only he could.

Leadership is a relay race. Even the longest-lasting college presidents are only in place for a small fraction of the life of their college. (Toward the end of my decade at Maryville, we celebrated the school's bicentennial, which certainly put things in perspective.) I always approach leadership positions as temporary; therefore I emphasize building structures and preparing people who could successfully carry on after I am gone. I see far too little of this mindset in higher education. My impression is that for-profit corporations are more intentional about succession planning than colleges, but that might be due to me looking for models rather than a true picture of the entire environment.

If one is working to build up other leaders, a natural corollary is that it is vital to allow those other people to make decisions. And of course, other people will make decisions that differ from mine—sometimes for the better, sometimes not. No matter how difficult it is, I need to allow others to make decisions. This lesson, too, I originally took from a book—in this case, *Dune* by Frank Herbert (1965), which I first read back in high school. The protagonist, being trained to become a great leader, is told, "Give as few orders as possible. . . . Once you've given orders on a subject, you must always give orders on that subject" (387). This was one lesson, at least, that I was able to learn the easy way, by reading, instead of the hard way through painful experience.

Everything I've said to this point is generic, in the sense that it doesn't apply only to small colleges. So why have I gravitated to small colleges? Another book explains it. In *Mr. Roberts*, by Thomas Heggen (1946 [1966]), the title character is a respected, popular, and effective officer on a cargo ship during WWII. But he longs to be where the action is, serving in combat, even though he could easily continue on his existing path. I already mentioned the ethos of creating value central to the Weatherhead School of Management. Taking that ethos seriously and personally led me to work at schools that are one semester away from a crisis. While the stakes are not as high as leading people in combat, there is nevertheless the reality that institutional survival might be at stake in a way that is not true at well-endowed institutions of high reputation.

As I was wrapping up my time at Maryville College, I had the opportunity to interview for the presidency of a well-known liberal arts college. The usual trajectory for a second presidency is to move "up the food chain" of the U. S. News ranking, and this would have been such a move. I noticed in my research about the institution that it struggled with enrollment but was located next to a thriving community college. One obvious (to me) step was to change the transfer-hostile core curriculum to something more attractive to students. My advocacy for such a step, while not finding a receptive audience, was not the death knell of my candidacy. That came during lunch with the trustees. The night before my campus visit, the board chair had told me that what mattered was having a higher U.S. News ranking than their rival, and I should be prepared to address that question at lunch. When the question came, I was prepared. I told them that to the extent that U.S. News valued measures that reflected the school accomplishing its mission, I welcomed their praise, but that pursuing U.S. News rankings for their own sake was not fruitful. I literally watched the room transform from excitement about a potential future president to an embarrassed scramble to finish up. I don't claim any particular virtue, other than being willing to seriously consider what I value and being willing to publicly articulate it. My second presidency, according to U.S. News, was a step down the food chain. However, their version of what's important and mine don't agree, and I'm proud of the work we were able to accomplish together at Columbia College.

Students approaching graduation often express to me the desire to stay in college just a little longer. My response is typically to agree via a little dad joke: I enjoyed college so much that I turned pro, so that rather than me paying to be in school, now the school pays me. They chuckle and move on, but I'm not really joking. The chance to be surrounded and challenged by talented people is an incredible privilege that I have never taken for granted. I didn't intend to become a college president. But having done it, I can't imagine wanting to take a different path.

One Semester Away from a Crisis

1

Introduction

Small colleges are a vital component of the United States' higher education system. However, their unique characteristics are often overlooked in analyses that incorporate all colleges and universities. For example, how do the distinctive features of small college finances and their workforce both constrain the choices they make and create possibilities different from those available at larger institutions?

Many concepts familiar to economics professors but less familiar to more general audiences are helpful in understanding small colleges. These concepts include sophisticated ideas not typically covered in basic economics courses, such as regulatory capture, decision-making under uncertainty, and the logic of collective action. By combining economic theories with my own experiences leading small colleges, I provide a way for presidents, trustees, and other leaders of small colleges to more effectively help their institutions achieve their full potential.

The book is written for leaders of small colleges, broadly defined. Presidents of small colleges are the clearest group of interested readers. Trustees can also benefit from better understanding the institutions they are stewarding. People who hold leadership positions at small colleges, whether or not they aspire to the presidency, will find this book helpful in their roles. It is also possible that this book will be a helpful asset for courses in higher education leadership. There are many textbooks and many memoirs, but there are not many books written from personal experience through an analytical lens. As we'll also see, many of the issues that affect small colleges are also present in regional public universities and even flagship public universities.

There has never been an easy time to be a leader of a small college. Leading these schools is challenging, as they are indeed "one semester away from a crisis." If the president, the board of trustees, or other leaders make poor decisions that lead to a loss of enrollment and enrollment-driven revenue, they can go out of business quickly. Small colleges typically have an endowment that provides only a small fraction of their budget, making them extremely vulnerable to any setback. The current set of existential crises facing enrollment-driven institutions is just the latest of those that have been publicly proclaimed by various voices for decades.

While the book draws on my personal experience as a small college leader, it is not a memoir. In some cases, I provide specific examples of how the economic concepts apply in a situation. But more often, I speak about general issues facing small colleges. Specific issues and their resolutions always have a context, including the available resources and details about personalities and policies, that limit their complete transferability to a new setting. But the specific issues are manifestations of enduring universal challenges. Because I have served as a president, I have heard a lot of presidents, trustees, and other campus leaders describe their challenges and their approaches to successfully addressing them. This knowledge, combined with my own experiences, informs the topics in the book, ensuring the ideas are immediately applicable for a wide range of readers. Although I regularly refer to specific schools and policy discussions, I recognize that the examples are out of date as soon as I write them. I use the examples to illustrate and motivate concepts that are useful much more broadly than the specific setting in which they are introduced.

Why "one semester away from a crisis?" One day I was congratulating a friend of mine who owns coffee shops on opening a new location and asked him how opening day went. He replied that "every day is opening day" for him. He considered himself one day away from a crisis, because if people don't show up, his business is in jeopardy. For enrollment-driven colleges, the analogous point is that if students don't arrive next semester, the institution is in jeopardy. No matter how well things went this semester, there is no guarantee that next semester will unfold positively.

After completing the book, the reader will have a new perspective on familiar issues. This will help provide them with "the wisdom to know the difference" between what can be changed and what cannot. They will also be better able to understand why some types of interventions are more challenging than they seem and why some types of seemingly counterintuitive actions might be sensible. Because every institution faces unique circumstances, the reader is not given a comprehensive to-do list or set of answers. Instead, they are equipped to engage effectively in their own context.

Which Colleges Are We Talking About?

I will tend to use "small college" and "teaching college" interchangeably. There are thousands of higher education institutions in the United States, no two of which are alike. Any taxonomy, therefore, is arbitrary in certain ways. The colleges and universities that are my focus share two and a half characteristics.

The first common characteristic is that the schools derive the bulk of their revenue from student enrollment. This includes tuition, fees, room and board, and other auxiliary services. Most institutions have some endowment earnings, philanthropic giving, and government or foundation grants. But for the schools I'm considering, their existence depends fundamentally on successfully enrolling students. At Columbia College during my tenure, for example, over 80 percent of total revenue was generated by tuition, fees, room, and board.

The second common characteristic is that the primary focus for the faculty is teaching undergraduate students. When I first joined Case Western Reserve University, about 10,000 students were enrolled, only about one-third of whom were undergraduates. By contrast, Maryville College enrolled only undergraduates from its founding in 1819 until creating its first graduate program in 2022, including my decade as president from 2010 through 2020. Faculty at Maryville and similar schools are typically expected to engage in some sort of scholarly activity or other professional development, but they are recruited and evaluated primarily on their ability to teach.

The final characteristic halfway shared is that the institutions are private. My leadership experience has been exclusively in so-called independent colleges, organized as nonprofit corporations with a self-perpetuating board. However, the opportunities and challenges at many state colleges and universities are very similar to those at small private teaching colleges. I am not speaking about the flagship research universities but about the other schools, including former teacher preparation institutions and branch campuses of state systems. While much of their revenue derives from the state government, it is typically tied very closely to enrollment, and the faculty recruitment and evaluation system typically resembles that in private teaching colleges: hence the "half."

What about small? That adjective is in the eye of the beholder. York College of Pennsylvania enrolled over 5,000 students while I was there, while Maryville College had about 1,150, and many colleges are even smaller. My experience is that the fundamental dynamics at York were not that different from Maryville. The typical enrollment cutoff identifying small colleges is 5,000. An informal test is whether the president can realistically know all the faculty and staff. If so, it is a small school. If the president can realistically know all the students, it's a very small school.

I believe that small colleges are a vital part of the vibrant higher education sector in the United States. Leading these schools is challenging, as they are indeed "one semester away from a crisis." That is perhaps the other dimension of "small" that distinguishes them. They have a small endowment or limited financial capacity more broadly. This sector is the main focus of those who regularly predict wholesale closures among colleges, a spectator sport that dates at least to the early 1980s. "A specter is haunting higher education: the specter of decline and bankruptcy. Experts predict that between 10 percent and 30 percent of America's 3,100 colleges and universities will close their doors or merge with other institutions by 1995" (Keller, 1983, 3). Those who have taken on the responsibility of proving these predictions wrong need all the analytical tools possible to help them better understand their situation and lead their institutions successfully.

Economics? Really?

I have observed through the years that many people did not enjoy studying economics or even avoided it altogether. Criticisms include perceived unreality of assumptions underlying economic analysis, lack of unanimity among economists about fundamental issues, perceived conservative political bias, and seeming arrogance among professional economists who invaded the topics studied in other social sciences. While pleading guilty at least in part to some of these criticisms, I nevertheless maintain that an economic perspective is useful in understanding higher education, especially for those who are charged with leading small colleges.

Economics, at its best, does not prescribe answers to any given situation. Rather, it provides a set of questions to ask along with a set of analytical and empirical tools for answering those questions. The questions, and sometimes the answers to them that result, can seem counterintuitive to people trained in other disciplines. This doesn't make economics right, but it does mean that economic analysis can add dimensions to the discussion.

The most important perspective that economics brings is the necessity of choice. Economists assume that resources are always scarce, which in turn implies that choice is always needed. A person's priorities can be inferred, in part, from the choices they make about how to use the scarce resources available to them. This leads me to be unsympathetic when institutions talk about having to rearrange plans because they ran out of money before they could finish a project. At two different institutions I served, for example, I was told about how a previous building project had to be curtailed because the funds ran out. This is not a tragedy; it is a dereliction of duty. In fact, this issue is well addressed in Luke's Gospel (14:28–30): "For which of you, intending to build a tower, sitteth not down first, and counteth the cost, whether he have sufficient to finish it? Lest haply, after he hath laid the foundation, and is not able to finish it, all that behold it begin to mock him, Saying, This man began to build, and was not able to finish."

As that example suggests, I regularly found that my immediate reaction to a variety of topics is very different from my colleagues who are not economists. For example, I am not surprised by the persistence of tuition discounting, even among institutions that claim to oppose it. I'll outline why in chapter 5. Economic analysis also explains why faculty members are so invested in the importance of shared governance and how the process that leads to people becoming faculty members implies that it will be difficult to revise the core curriculum (chapter 7). Economic analysis is not the only perspective to take. But it is a useful perspective I am familiar with that most people aren't. That seems like a nice opportunity for me to be helpful.

A desirable feature of economic analysis is that it treats every person as autonomous rather than as an instrument to carry out instructions. People are ends, rather than means. No matter what curriculum a college develops, students will look for ways to enroll in the courses they want to take. No matter what activities a college wants them to pursue, students will look for ways to create the clubs they want and spend time playing the games they enjoy. No matter what the dean dictates, the faculty will look to pursue their own intellectual interests. Because economists respect that every person is making choices, we approach policy decisions with a recognition that people will look for loopholes. While this complicates simple answers to difficult questions, it also brings the potential for lasting solutions to chronic problems.

Who's in Charge? A Model of College Leadership

Economists use models as a tool of analysis. A model is a deliberate simplification of reality that makes it possible to develop hypotheses and to analyze whether predictions match outcomes. While economists are often pilloried for unrealistic models, this criticism is unfounded to the extent it is narrowly focused on models not being comprehensive. None of us can truly develop a model that includes all information, not even in the new age of generative artificial intelligence. As the statistician George Box famously said, "All models are wrong, but some are useful."

Because the intended audience of this book are leaders of small colleges, I want to introduce a model of small college governance, based on one originally developed by Ed Glaeser (2002). This model is both a chance to see how economists think and a model that will recur in discussions of some specific questions later in the book. This is the only time in the book that anything resembling algebra or math will appear. While that may dismay economists, who enjoy writing down mathematical models, it will likely be welcome news to most people.

The question of who is in charge of a college is complicated. In the model, there are four groups that plausibly can claim to govern the direction of a college: students, faculty/staff, administration/board, and donors/alumni.

Suppose that we can describe a college by a number, X, that is between 0 and 1. Further, suppose that students prefer a lower X than faculty/staff. For example, X could denote a college's position on the axis of "career-focused" (0) to "liberal arts" (1), "party school" to "academic," "teaching" to "research," or "religious" to "secular." The amount that students are willing to pay to attend the school will depend on how close X is to their preferred point. If students differ from each other in their preferred type of school, then it is possible that they choose schools that have different X.

Faculty happiness depends on how large X is, with 1 being the preferred value. The amount of salary required to attract a faculty member will also depend on X, with a lower salary being possible if X is higher, all else being equal.

The management (administration/board) cares about how many students are served while balancing the budget. Managers also have a preferred level of X and will move the school toward that level if they can. Although faculty do not directly set the level of X, they have the ability to inflict costs on management if X is decreased. The most dramatic example of such a cost is a no-confidence vote.

Finally, to highlight the potential for conflict between donors and faculty, suppose that donors prefer that X equals 0 and donors give less as X is increased. The challenge for management in this framework is how to achieve their preferred outcome (high enrollment and preferred level of X) while balancing the budget. The revenue from donors is higher if X is lower, and the revenue from students is higher if X is close to their preferences. On the other hand, the costs are lower if X is higher, both because the amount required to pay faculty/staff goes down and the costs to management imposed by faculty/staff are lower.

What is the outcome? It will depend both on the exact preferences of the various groups and on their relative bargaining power. The general point, though—that managers face a challenging problem in balancing the preferences of various constituents—is one that will be familiar to anyone in a leadership role. We can also frame the choice of president as one of finding someone with a preferred value of X that is the best compromise among the various other groups. And while the flattening of institutional characteristics to one dimension removes nuance, it also clarifies the idea of what it means for a person to be a good fit for a college.

Plan of the Book

The rest of the book introduces more economic concepts and illustrates how they can be helpful in understanding and leading teaching colleges. Most of the chapters are self-contained, so you should feel free to jump to topics that you find most interesting or relevant. Because this is an attempt to connect economic concepts with issues facing small colleges, I do not attempt to comprehensively treat each subject. If you get hooked on economics, there are a lot of good books out there that systematically explore the ideas. I conclude the book with Suggestions for Further Reading, listing a few of the books that I have found most helpful.

In chapter 2 (Make vs. Buy), I begin with one of the core areas of economic analysis: when to buy from someone else instead of doing it yourself. This lets us explore both the basics about how economists analyze choices and more sophisticated concepts such as principal-agent problems and incomplete contracts. Essentially, the point is that deciding to purchase a good or service is not the end of the process but rather just the beginning. I pay close attention to the choice facing the student in whether to attend college or not, as it is the defining question for small colleges.

Chapter 3 (Friends, Rivals, Neighbors, and Family) reviews some examples of how schools that seem to be in competition with each other are also cooperating with each other. A pervasive misconception among people who do not work in higher education is that the schools are perennially in conflict and involved in zero-sum competition. While there are examples of this situation, it is more common that they are pursuing complementary goals and looking for mutually beneficial opportunities. This analytical lens provides a counterintuitive view regarding the benefits to small colleges of free community college programs. The chapter also presents a model of alumni engagement that explains why people are motivated to volunteer for selfish reasons as well as for altruistic ones.

One broadly familiar idea from personal finance is that of a balanced portfolio. Chapter 4 (Portfolio) explains what the benefits of a portfolio are as well as clarifying the key characteristic of a balanced portfolio. Portfolio theory applies not only to a college's endowment and other investments but also to its academic programs and geographic outreach.

Having brought up investments, which is a clear link between the nonprofit world of higher education and the for-profit world of business, in chapter 5 (Making a Profit), the emphasis is on understanding nonprofit education as a business. Some common practices in higher education, including tuition discounting and requiring students to live on campus, are best understood as efforts to make sure that revenue exceeds cost, even when there are seemingly plausible alternative explanations.

Chapter 6 (One Semester Away from a Crisis) focuses on the impact on decision-making of small colleges being extremely constrained. The logic behind some seemingly suboptimal choices, including widespread deferred maintenance and one-sided public–private partnerships, becomes clear once the nature and extent of the constraints is understood. This is not to say that every decision made by a small college is correct. Rather, the point is that decisions are shaped not only by what people want but also by what is possible.

In chapter 7 (Secular Missionaries), the focus turns to the faculty and staff who work at small colleges. One feature of higher education, the emphasis on shared governance, emerges as a feature of the recruitment process and the job market instead of as an exogenously determined characteristic. Given that many trustees and many college presidents who come from outside academia struggle to effectively function in a shared governance environment, a better understanding of its causes is vital.

The world is full of unknowns, and economists spend a great deal of time systematically analyzing the various types of unknowns and their implications. Chapter 8 (Risk and Uncertainty) uses the contrast between risk ("known unknowns") and uncertainty ("unknown unknowns") as a launching point for investigating questions ranging from faculty hiring to admissions materials.

In a world of unknowns, people are drawn to information providers. Chapter 9 (Herding) describes how colleges in an uncertain world tend to herd—that is, to make similar decisions and communicate in similar ways. This tendency is reinforced by college rankings, which are a zero-sum counterexample to my general observation about the cooperative environment of higher education.

Higher education is a highly regulated industry, including regulations from Federal, state, and local governments, as well as self-imposed regulators (accreditation). Certain aspects of regulation are best understood as attempts by the regulated group to raise barriers that prevent the entry of potential competitors. In chapter 10 (Regulation), this idea is expanded upon using examples such as program accreditation and teacher licensure. More broadly, some of the challenges of imposing a single regulatory structure on a heterogeneous sector are explored.

Chapter 11 (Mergers, Consortia, Startups, and Closures) looks at the future of small colleges. It analyzes the persistent question of why more small colleges don't merge or close, which has been an active area of inquiry for decades. An important part of the explanation is found in the nature of most colleges as nonprofit organizations, which creates incentives that differ from the situation with for-profit organizations. One explanation for the survival of small colleges is found in thinking carefully about why students enroll there, which brings us full circle to the reason that these colleges exist at all. An uncomfortable question that is not often asked is considered—if small colleges are so great, why don't more start?

2

Make vs. Buy

Economists get a bad rap. We are usually viewed at best as resembling Ambrose Bierce's definition of a cynic in the Devil's Dictionary (1906 [1958], 27): "A blackguard whose faulty vision sees things as they are, not as they ought to be." And as much as it pains me, there is some truth to this description.

Economics overlaps with other fields of study, with insights from psychology being one of the important areas of growth in recent decades. One of the standard assumptions in economics is that human wants are unlimited. In the words of the author of Ecclesiastes (4:8), "Their eyes are never satisfied with riches." That is an extreme view, and a natural question is how true it is. One robust finding of researchers takes the following form. Ask people two questions. First, how much money does it take for you to live comfortably? Second, how much money would it take for you to be completely happy? The answer to the first question is approximately their current income. The answer to the second question is typically two to three times their current income. If your income is $20,000, you think that $40,000 will be plenty; if your income is $40,000, you think that $80,000 will be plenty; and so on. This is certainly a case where academic research and Biblical wisdom share a similar conclusion.

But I'm not here to be completely depressing, so I want to turn to a more optimistic take on this topic. In graduate school, Professor

Hugo Sonnenschein provided a memorable metaphor for how economists think about the world. He described a dream in which he first traveled to Hell. In his dream, Hell was described as an incredible banquet with every possible delicious food. The catch, though, was that while each person could reach the food, they could not move their arms to bring the food to their mouths. The result was a chaotic scene of frustration and anger. Next in his dream he traveled to Heaven. Amazingly enough, Heaven had exactly the same setup—an incredible feast with each person unable to feed themselves. The difference, though, is that in Heaven people fed each other. Economists see the world as a series of opportunities for mutually beneficial relationships. Most of our professional energy is spent on market relationships, where the mutual benefit is between willing buyers and willing sellers. But attention also goes to volunteering and other forms of nonmarket (or at least nonmonetary) activity.

Because economists recognize that nothing is free, we are accused of lacking a heart. But even the most famous literary character who lacked a heart understood how to compensate for that lack.

The Tin Woodsman knew very well he had no heart, and therefore he took great care never to be cruel or unkind to anything. "You people with hearts," he said, "have something to guide you, and need never do wrong; but I have no heart, and so I must be very careful" (Baum, 1900 [1979], 75).

Yes, there is always cost, but that doesn't mean we don't appreciate net benefits—even benefits that can't be expressed in monetary terms. Economists, with their emphasis on mutual advantage, are not the terrible cynics of stereotype but rather realistic searchers for improvement.

Comparative Advantage

Small colleges, almost by definition, can't do everything for themselves. The question, then, is what they should do themselves and what they should purchase from others. Given my insistence that economists see the world through the lens of mutually beneficial arrangements, you'll be unsurprised to know that there is a fundamental analytical tool that can be used to figure out the question.

The concept is called comparative advantage. I'll start with a definition. A college has a comparative advantage in an activity if the opportunity cost of performing an activity at a given quality level is less than the cost of purchasing it. That's fine, but it leads to the need to define opportunity cost.

The opportunity cost of an activity or a product is the value of the next best alternative use of the resources used to obtain the product or do the activity. Here is where true economic analysis diverges from the caricature of economists only caring about money. The resources used include not only money but also time. And the benefits and costs of a good or service are not only financial, but they can include intangible factors like how you feel about the way the good was obtained. What matters to economists is the net benefit—the benefits received from the good or service minus the (opportunity) cost. That's why I specified a given level of quality in defining comparative advantage.

Let's start with a familiar situation. I'm considering a small home repair project. I could hire a contractor to do it, and it would take them three hours for which they would charge me $500. Alternatively, I could do it myself. This would only cost $100, but it would take me ten hours. Why the difference? First, I would have to spend a couple of hours watching YouTube videos to learn how to do the work and make two trips to Home Depot to purchase materials. (The second trip is because I hadn't realized exactly what I needed.) I would also wind up owning a tool needed for the job that I am unlikely to ever use again and must find storage space for. Which approach is less expensive?

The correct answer to any question asked by an economist is, "It depends." In this case, it depends on (at least) three factors. The first factor is my willingness to trade off money for time. In this example, I save $400 by doing the work myself but give up ten hours of my time. That's $40 per hour. It is tempting to just compare that to my hourly wage. But given that I wouldn't be doing the home project during the time I'm doing my job, it's not obvious what the right cost per hour should be. It depends on what I would do with that time if I didn't undertake the repair. And if I enjoy doing home repair, the "cost" might even be negative, in that I'd be willing to pay a certain amount of money to do the work. The second factor is the quality of the final product. What matters, after all, is not only the cost of the project but how well the house functions afterwards. If I do the work less expensively but the result is poorly functioning or unattractive, then the true "cost" of doing it myself is greater than just the money and time. A third factor is the pleasure I get from accomplishing something myself rather than having someone else do the work. Suppose that the quality of the work is identical whether I do it myself or hire someone. I might derive added pleasure from the knowledge that I did the work myself or from future opportunities to brag to others about the project. How much this pleasure matters will vary from person to person and even from project to project.

Given that even a relatively simple example includes some complications, it is unsurprising that the best answer for actual situations facing college leaders is not easy to determine. Consider the activity of feeding students who live on campus. One approach would be to hire a food service company to construct space, obtain food, prepare and serve the food, and clean up afterwards. A second approach would be to construct the space and then hire a company to prepare and serve the food. A third approach would be for the college to construct the space, hire employees, and prepare and serve the food itself. All three of these approaches are used by some colleges, along with variations on these basic themes.

There are a variety of costs and benefits involved in evaluating which of these three approaches is right for your college at this time. But suppose you have an existing kitchen and dining hall, so the question of building a structure is not relevant. Then the choice is whether to hire a company or to do the work yourself. For the sake of the analysis, suppose that the quality of the food and service is identical. In that case, evaluating the opportunity cost boils down to figuring out whether it is less expensive to hire an outside company or do it yourself.

Typically, though, the question is not that simple, for reasons like those we saw in the example of a home repair project. It might be the case that an outside company has purchasing power that lets it obtain food at a lower price but at the cost of a menu that is not as targeted to the desires of the campus community. Alternatively, an outside company might bring expertise that would be difficult for a small college to replicate, and so on. The key, to an economist, is to realize that by choosing one approach, you have given up something in order to obtain something else. Should you do it yourself or hire someone else? The answer is whichever most effectively advances your mission.

I have used the example of food service, but the basic principle applies to a multitude of situations, large and small. Create your own online program or partner with a company that specializes in online programs? Produce a marketing brochure using college staff or hire a local (or national) design company? Purchase and maintain printers or lease them from a company that also services them?

The question of whether to do something yourself or hire someone else is not only fundamental to college operations but also precisely the question that each potential student faces, and we now turn to that issue.

Why Enroll in College?

Having defined small colleges as enrollment-driven, the existential question for them is whether students will enroll. While perhaps in prior years the advantages of enrolling in college to obtain an education were so self-evident as to not require analysis, that is no longer the public sentiment. Given the ubiquity of information courtesy of the internet, especially with the added curatorial element of artificial intelligence, a person can readily put together a program of self-education rather than purchasing the education from a school.

The costs of enrolling in college are substantial. There are obvious financial costs for tuition. There are also more subtle costs such as the opportunity cost of foregone employment. We have already met opportunity cost, and it is the fundamental concept in economics that makes concrete the idea that nothing is free. The time spent studying and attending class could have been spent working, and the money that could have been earned is a cost even though it is not visible. Another subtle cost is that the geographic location of the school that best fits a student might not be the preferred geography for the student. A familiar example is the student who must move away from their significant other in a long-distance relationship. Another cost is found in the case of students who are the first (or among the first) in their family and community to attend college. The change in professional prospects, relationships, and even clothing and language can lead to awkwardness and even alienation from the student's previous home without necessarily making them fully part of their new world. The challenge of moving to a substantially different social class is not a new situation, as the experience of the title character in *The Great Gatsby* (along with many other examples from literature) illustrates (Fitzgerald, 1925). The denouement of *The Great Gatsby* also illustrates how high the stakes can be both for the person moving and for those they left behind.

There must be some benefits, then, to justify a student choosing to enroll in a college. If we stipulate that the student can obtain a good education without attending college—not an uncontested assertion—then we must look elsewhere for benefits that exceed the costs articulated previously. One important benefit is, in fact, the social network that is developed and reinforced in college. Alumni associations are a manifest version of this advantage, as they usually emphasize the opportunities for networking and mentoring that favor current students as well as graduates of their school.

Another feature in the United States social structure has been the rise in assortative mating that has mirrored the increase in female academic and professional accomplishment. To put it crudely, where once a lawyer married his secretary, now a doctor might marry her fellow medical student. While there are reasons to be concerned about the resulting reinforcement of class divisions, for an individual there can be advantages in both financial and social terms from this phenomenon.

A standard argument for college attendance is the higher salary obtained as a result. Interestingly, though, this outcome is mostly restricted to those who graduate from college rather than just attending college. This phenomenon is called the "sheepskin effect," and it poses questions as to exactly how the student benefits from their time in college. If the benefits are purely from learning material and skills, then we would expect an increase in salary for each year of school completed. Instead, the pattern is essentially no increase at all until after graduation. This is consistent with the idea that what happens at college is that the student signals to potential future employers that they can successfully navigate a bureaucracy and that they are willing to devote years to working hard before receiving a payoff. These are traits that employers value.

Principal-Agent Issues

Suppose you've decided to purchase goods and services from others rather than try to do everything yourself. How can you be sure that you are getting your money's worth when you buy? Remember the fundamental axiom in economics—people are trying to make themselves as happy as possible. Work is difficult, and delivering high-quality goods and services is difficult. Won't people be tempted to rip you off by not working hard and by delivering low-quality goods and services? Of course they will. Or perhaps faculty and staff will proselytize for their favored religious, political, or cultural cause rather than providing the high-quality education that a student is looking for. (This is a concern that the political system pays a great deal of attention to.) Or the college will emphasize broad-based liberal arts education rather than specific job skills, which might reflect different ideas from their students and their families about what a high-quality education entails. Fortunately, economists have been thinking carefully about how to solve this conundrum for a long time.

The situation in economics is called the "principal–agent problem." A principal is someone who wants something, and the agent is someone hired to provide it. For example, a car owner could be a principal who wants their car serviced and the mechanic an agent. Or a college that wants its facilities maintained can be the principal and the company it hires to do so the agent. Principal–agent problems are pervasive, as these examples suggest. There are three general approaches to solving them. First, carefully monitor the agent. Second, compensate the agent based on performance. Third, use competitive pressures to provide appropriate incentives for the agent. (Technically there is a fourth answer: make the principal the agent. "If you want something done right, do it yourself." But that can't be a general answer for a small college, although it is the example for an individual student—educating themself—we discussed previously.)

When people are posed the principal–agent problem, the initial reaction is generally to propose some form of monitoring. And it's logical to start there. If we keep an eye on the situation, then the agent won't be able to deliver less than we want. But remember: nothing is free. While we're monitoring the agent, we are giving up the opportunity to do something else worthwhile. Aha! We can hire someone to watch the agent. But then we've just increased the cost of the activity and added a second principal–agent problem to the mix (how do you know your monitor is doing a good job?). Further, as the car mechanic example illustrates, there are times when we might not be able to distinguish whether the agent is doing a good job or not. If my college lacks the internal expertise to provide IT infrastructure, how can I be sure that my IT provider is doing a good job? Is that person staring out the window thinking deep thoughts about an important issue or just daydreaming? Finally, the agent might resent the monitoring and change their behavior accordingly. If I rigorously monitor how long a lunch break lasts to be sure that the employee isn't slacking off, they might well decide to make sure that they always take their entire lunch break rather than sometimes cutting it short to address urgent matters.

These drawbacks to direct monitoring lead to the next set of approaches, which work to align the incentives of the principal and the agent. The classic example is performance-based compensation, whether in the form of sharecropping (described by Xenophon in his study of Athens about 2500 years ago), stock options (which turn an employee into an owner, thus aligning their incentives), or bonuses based on achieving performance goals. Stock options are not possible in a nonprofit college setting, but performance-based compensation is still possible. For example, a contractor can be hired for a construction project for a guaranteed maximum price, and if the project is delivered (at the requisite quality) for less than that price, the contractor can receive a portion of the savings. Excellent employees can be rewarded with bonuses; outstanding teachers can earn awards. One challenge with performance-based compensation is that it forces the agent to bear some of the risk. That, in turn, might increase the cost to the college because it has to compensate the agent for bearing the risk. Another challenge is that specifying outcomes that will be rewarded creates an incentive for the agent to focus on achieving those outcomes, perhaps to the detriment of truly accomplishing the principal's goal. The familiar criticism of "teaching to the test" in the case of high-stakes assessment measures is one example of this possibility.

In addition to the element of risk, designing performance-based compensation can be complicated. The final general approach to solving the principal–agent problem abstracts one more level and focuses on the environment in which the agent operates. The basic idea is that there are often multiple agents available to be hired and that multiple principals will want to hire them over time. One source of information is the reputation that an agent has earned based on their previous performance. The proliferation of online reviews has made this angle quite familiar, but word-of-mouth and reference checking are old habits that are still relevant today. Another source of information is provided when multiple agents are invited to bid on a project. Even if I don't know the right questions to ask of the agent, they will want to educate me about how their approach is superior to that of their competitors. This general question of learning about the environment is one that we will return to in chapter 8.

Incomplete Contracts

To this point, much of the discussion has implicitly assumed that every relevant part of the agent's performance can be identified. But education, in common with many other services, deals with outcomes that are difficult to observe and sometimes even difficult to define. Just about every college claims to prepare students to be lifelong learners. How does one measure this outcome? And how does one hold faculty and staff accountable for achieving it, given that the outcome is, by definition, unobservable until the student has lived their entire life?

Anticipating the discussion in chapter 3, the challenge of agreeing on every aspect of a partnership is also daunting. No matter how diligently and honestly we work to predict possible scenarios and agree to address them, we will be faced with unexpected situations. This adds another layer of complexity to the situation. If we ask the college's attorney, they will recommend adding stipulations to address every contingency. But that is impossible, and spending too much time and effort focused on everything that can go wrong could end up undermining the work or even preventing the partnership from occurring.

What is to be done? That is not an easy question, and in fact Oliver Hart won a Nobel Prize in 2016 for his work both in formulating the question and helping to develop some answers. In general, the answer is to build a strong working relationship built on trust. One element of building the relationship is to set limits on what is included in the collaboration. Agreeing to accept transfer credits in a specific program is a much different proposition than agreeing to synchronize curricula across institutions. Working with a nearby college to create a joint educational center in a downtown building is difficult, but specific, when compared to merging two colleges.

Beyond being specific about the area of collaboration, another key is to develop an effective process for making joint decisions. There is a cliché about emergencies—you shouldn't be exchanging business cards during a hurricane. The point is that plans should have been developed before the emergency, including building relationships among the individuals and institutions and determining a structure for responding to whatever contingency arises.

The largest emergency I dealt with as a president was the COVID-19 pandemic. At Maryville College, about 75 percent of the students lived on campus, all of whom participated in the meal plan. We had chosen to purchase food service from another company. When we sent all the students home in March 2020, we also committed to a prorated refund of room and board costs (even before the Federal government announced it would help). We asked our food service provider to share in the financial challenge this would entail by accepting a reduced payment from us for the semester. A worldwide pandemic was well outside the usual scope of contract negotiations. Fortunately, because we had worked closely over the years and been transparent with each other, there was a reservoir of trust to draw on. We quickly reached an agreement that fairly shared the pain.

Although this discussion has moved beyond the basic principal–agent problem, let's conclude by noting that incomplete contracts plague principal–agent relationships as well. When hiring people or companies, it is crucial not only to consider how to align the incentives of the agent with those of the principal but also to build trust and develop a process for making decisions in situations that aren't explicitly covered by the contract.

Students as Principals

By choosing to enroll in college, a student takes on the role of the principal in a principal–agent relationship with the college. How, then, do the basic theoretical ideas of how to solve a principal–agent problem play out in this important setting?

First, consider monitoring. The student wants something out of their college education, which is not necessarily the same thing the college (in the form of its faculty and staff) wants to provide. Theoretically, the student could specify what they expect to be delivered to them. The idea of incomplete contracts suggests this might be challenging, even if the student knows exactly what they want. However, one definition of a good education is that it helps the student become part of a larger world than before they were educated. In that case, it might be difficult for the student to accurately predict exactly what outcome they want, as the process of education itself will reveal their true preferences. However, a better understanding of the types of results that other students have received can at least provide some general idea about the benefits of a particular school. While I don't have a lot of good things to say about most ranking systems and college scorecards, this is one of the places where there is at least a theoretical justification for them.

Second, what about aligning incentives? The clearest example of such a program is the so-called LRAP, which stands for Loan Repayment Assistance Program. This type of program generally includes some sort of guarantee for a student. For example, if a student borrows money to attend college, graduates, and earns a salary less than a given amount, then the student is not responsible for repaying their loan. This provides the school with a financial incentive to make sure the student earns a salary above the minimum. More broadly, the more students respond to information in college scorecards and rankings that focus on student outcomes such as graduation rates, job placement rates, and salaries, the more colleges will feel the need to score well on those outcomes. (There is a negative side to this incentive, as we will see in chapter 9.) The ultimate sanction behind most government regulation is the potential loss of Federal financial aid for students, which is a financial death sentence for enrollment-driven institutions. The implicit justification for such a structure is to make sure that schools emphasize what the government wants in its role as funding student enrollment. (The principal–agent problem with the government as principal in its role as funder of college education and student as agent is left as an exercise for the reader. There is an important analog to healthcare, in that the person who benefits is not necessarily the person who is paying the bill.)

Third is the competitive environment. Here is, once again, a place where rankings and scorecards loom large. Colleges spend incredible amounts of resources explaining why their institution is better than others. A careful student can learn much about what other people think are the key components of a college education by comparing the common dimensions in which colleges claim to excel. I would be hard-pressed to find a school, no matter how large, that doesn't claim to prioritize small classes and close interaction between students and faculty. Unfortunately, though, the fact that everyone makes the same claim makes it difficult to distinguish which institution is truly the best fit. An important challenge here is the heterogeneity of both students and colleges. Even if I learn that students who seem similar to me have enjoyed a good experience at a school, that does not guarantee that I will also enjoy a good experience.

Students as Agents

A recurring idea is that students attend college to improve their employment opportunities and career prospects. And because there is considerable evidence that employers value students attending college, it raises the question about what those benefits are. One lens of analyzing this question is to consider the future employer as a principal employing the student as an agent.

The popular mantra "do what you love" has a special resonance in the context of a principal–agent problem. It sounds a lot like aligning the incentives of the principal and the agent. If the principal values producing high-quality audits and the agent loves auditing, then there's a greater chance that the agent will perform to the principal's expectations.

As already alluded to, a slightly more sinister interpretation can be drawn from employers preferring to hire college graduates. In this telling, some people are more willing to work hard for low or deferred rewards than other people. It's true that a standard undergraduate college education involves challenging academic work, but it also requires obeying a complicated set of rules and navigating a bureaucracy both to attend and to finance college. Thus, an employer knows that someone who has graduated from college is willing to work hard and has learned how to follow rules. This reduces the likelihood that they are an agent who will shirk what the principal wants done.

The most diabolical economics story relates student debt to solving the principal–agent problem between employers and workers. The employer wants to know that it is hiring someone it can count on to work hard. One way for a hard worker to identify themselves is to provide a guarantee to the employer in the form of a deposit that is forfeited if they slack off. If not illegal, this is at least a challenging contract to write. However, consider a student who has taken on some student debt. Because this debt is permanent, in that it can't be discharged in bankruptcy, the employer knows that the student is motivated to succeed to earn money to repay the loan. To be clear, I'm not advocating for every student to take on debt to help ensure a motivated and productive workforce. But basic economic analysis implies that the fact that most students (about two-thirds of undergraduates) take on some debt can be interpreted by employers in a positive way.

Competition

Students compete for jobs, companies compete to hire employees, and colleges compete to recruit students and hire faculty and staff. The pervasiveness of competitive situations is reflected in the longstanding interest of economists in the outcomes of competition, beyond its role in ameliorating principal–agent problems.

One important outcome is that competition can provide benefits because companies try to provide goods and services that people are willing to pay for. Colleges provide not only a wide variety of academic disciplines to study but also a wide variety of environments in which to pursue those studies. As a result, students can more closely match their interests to what is provided than if there were a single approach.

A drawback of this variety is that it might be more expensive to provide many varieties than to focus on just one approach. The term "economies of scale" is used to describe when the cost per unit for a product decreases as the quantity produced goes up. These cost savings are most clearly seen in the case of asynchronous online education, where the initial investment in course development and administration can be spread over a large number of students at a small incremental cost. Around 2012, there was the belief that MOOCs (massive open online courses) would take advantage of these economies of scale and drive traditional in-person educational providers out of business. That hasn't happened, as students have gravitated to a variety of delivery approaches, both online and in-person.

If multiple providers are competing, then, all else being equal, they will be forced to sell at the lowest price they can afford while keeping their customers. Some companies will have a more desirable product, which will let them charge more. Some companies will have cost advantages, which will let them charge less. But all of them face some constraints, with the result that, at the margin, a company will make zero economic profit (that is, accounting for all opportunity costs). Similarly, at the margin, a student will pay exactly what they are willing to pay in order to attend school, while other students might receive a surplus. Faculty and staff face a similar dynamic as they search for their desired professional positions.

Is competition good or bad? It depends. Throughout the book, we will see ways in which competition provides both benefits and costs. Because it is impossible to definitively generalize, the specific situation must always be carefully analyzed before reaching a conclusion.

3

Friends, Rivals, Neighbors, and Family

Colleges operate in a fascinating environment. In addition to figuring out how to run their own school, leaders must navigate a world in which other people and institutions are making decisions that influence their success. Economists have devoted considerable attention to these sorts of strategic interactions. We concluded the previous chapter with some thoughts about competition. Despite the stereotype of economics focusing exclusively on competition, there is at least as much attention paid to when it makes sense to adopt a cooperative approach. Regardless of the situation, thinking clearly about the motivation and constraints of those with whom you interact can help you reach a better outcome.

Coopetition

Like many academics, I'm a sucker for a good neologism. Coopetition is a clear mash-up (or portmanteau word in Lewis Carroll's memorable phrasing) of cooperation and competition (Brandenburger and Nalebuff 2021). It is also a good description of the environment in which small colleges often operate. The key idea behind coopetition is that there can be mutually beneficial relationships even among rivals. One of the core insights of economics is the value and importance of mutually beneficial trade, but this is not always the default framing of interactions for people trained in other disciplines. There are exceptions, dating back at least as far as the author of Ecclesiastes (4:9–10) who says, "Two are better than one, because they have a good reward for their toil. For if they fall, one will lift up the other; but woe to one who is alone and falls and does not have another to help."

Some competitive situations are more easily seen as opportunities for cooperation than others. We'll start with a relatively straightforward example and work from there. The first case of coopetition is the athletic conference to which the college belongs. This example will clarify the ways that cooperation among rivals can be helpful to all of them. The second case of coopetition is trickier: the proximity of a major research university. The challenge to a small college of such a neighbor is clear, but there are also advantages. The third case is even more difficult and is one where my view differs considerably from most small college leaders. This is the public policy of free tuition for community colleges. Yes, there is clear competition for students that results, but there are also important opportunities for cooperation.

Athletic Conference

A familiar metaphor is that a college's athletic program is its front porch. It's not the most important part of the house, but it's visible and it's where people gather and are introduced to the house. Extending that metaphor, the athletic conference can be thought of as the neighborhood in which the college is located.

The competitive aspect of an athletic conference is clear. Teams compete with each other in athletic contests, with winners and losers, leading to outcomes that can include qualifying for regional or national competitions. In addition, the teams from each school compete to recruit the best students, which seems like a zero-sum environment. After all, if the basketball player or swimmer attends your college, they can't attend mine. So how is this a fertile ground for cooperation?

One answer lies in the elusive phrase "student experience." At enrollment-driven institutions, it is essential to recruit and retain students. Given the plethora of college options available, a student needs a reason to choose one college over another. Many (most?) students at small colleges are not there mainly for the academics but are instead looking for the opportunity to "do their thing," whether that be athletics, arts, spiritual life, or community service. The opportunity for a student to continue playing their sport at the college level, even if that opportunity doesn't come with an athletic scholarship as at large institutions, is a reason to attend.

Why, though, would a prospective student athlete choose one school over another? They will look at the facilities and coaching staff, to be sure, but a substantial reason will be the quality of competition. This is where belonging to the right conference matters. There are multiple dimensions of compatibility among schools in a conference that can enhance the student experience.

Although the huge athletic conferences such as the Southeastern Conference and the Big Ten get the lion's share of attention, most colleges do not belong to such sprawling entities. The travel required would be both academically and financially impossible to maintain. Therefore, it is vital to find a conference that covers a territory that helps the college. Ideally, the geography of the athletic conference should closely match the geography of the primary recruiting area for students. That makes it easier for family and friends to attend games and support the students, and it also keeps the college's name in local media in target markets.

A distinguishing feature of American higher education is the heterogeneity of educational institutions. Even within a relatively small geographical area, there will be schools of a variety of sizes with diverse missions. A student will not have a positive athletic experience if they are in a situation that is not competitive. Therefore, the ideal athletic conference will include schools of similar sizes and financial resources. One subtle benefit of institutional compatibility for a college president is the opportunity to build trusting relationships with other presidents. In one academic conference that I participated in, the presidents would engage in a general roundtable discussion after the conference business had been attended to. Because we were leading comparable institutions in a common region, we faced many similar challenges and could share our successes and failures as we worked together to strengthen our schools.

All colleges are academic, but not all colleges enroll students with the same academic profile. Even if the schools are compatible in size, finances, and geography, a mismatch in academics can lead to difficulties. All else being equal, the school that is more restrictive is at a disadvantage in recruiting. For example, compare a school that requires an ACT of 21 for admission with a school that requires an ACT of 24. The former school has a substantially larger pool of potential students, which can translate into a structural advantage in athletics, reducing the enjoyment of students at the latter school who know they are unlikely to ever win. This example is oversimplified for clarity, but it is nevertheless illustrative. An extreme example of an athletic conference emphasizing academic compatibility is the University Athletic Association, composed entirely of research universities. While the schools are not close to each other, covering a territory from Brandeis in Massachusetts to Washington University in St. Louis to Emory in Atlanta, all of them are compatible in their highly selective admissions and rigorous academic practices.

The Research University Next Door

Right after I arrived as president of Maryville College, I arranged to meet with the chancellor of the University of Tennessee,

Knoxville (UTK), a distinguished educator named Jimmy Cheek. The two schools are less than 20 miles apart, so it is easy to travel between them. I had a little speech ready with some reasons it would be great for us to cooperate: not every student is looking for a large school experience like that at UTK; many of Maryville's graduates went on to graduate and professional study at UTK; our talented faculty, staff, and students could complement the work being done at UTK. Imagine my shock when I walked into his office and, within about 30 seconds of greeting me, he gave my speech for me. Needless to say, we got along well and were able to further develop opportunities that joined the strengths of the two schools. Perhaps the one I'm proudest of was an accelerated path from undergraduate study to veterinary school, because veterinary schools are among the most selective programs in the country.

One advantage that large universities have over small colleges is the scope and scale of student activities available. These range from ROTC to social organizations to large-scale athletics to businesses serving students. An advantage that small colleges have over large universities is the personal scale of the operation, where students can get to know a significant portion of their classmates and where faculty and staff get to know students on an individual basis. Small colleges located close to a large university can credibly argue to students that they can truly enjoy the best of both worlds. Columbia College is a 5-mile drive up North Main Street from the University of South Carolina. Of course, we worked to build academic pipelines to their graduate programs, but we also helped students get tickets to football games, and we touted our proximity to the Five Points business area adjacent to the University of South Carolina campus as a great social opportunity for our students. This is a very different recruiting pitch than is available to a college that is located outside a metropolitan setting.

Proximity to a large university is helpful in recruiting not only students but also faculty and staff. Many academics marry each other, and it is not always easy for them to find jobs at the same institution. At both Maryville College and Columbia College, we were able to hire some extremely talented professionals whose spouse worked at another college or university. More broadly, by having a location in a metropolitan area, we were able to recruit people whose spouses were looking for employment because there was a good range of options available. While it is typically not possible for a college located in a rural area to move to a metropolitan area, it is nevertheless important to look for external partnerships, whether implicit or explicit, that can help attract and retain the highest quality people.

Free Community College

I once heard that the job of every college president is to take any piece of news and explain why it was the best possible news for their institution. Surely, the case of making community colleges tuition-free would strain even the most accomplished president of a small college. I don't know if I'm the most accomplished, but I will provide my reasoning about the benefits of such a program. This is not theoretical, as I experienced a zero-tuition program being introduced in Tennessee while I was president of Maryville College.

It seems obvious that reducing a college's tuition would make it more attractive to students. After all, in economics, if the price is reduced for a service (e.g., a community college education), then the quantity demanded should go up. And because some of that demand is reallocated from alternative services (e.g., a small private college education), then enrollment will drop in those places. I've stressed that enrollment is what drives the revenue for a small college, so how could losing enrollment possibly be a good thing?

Yes, it is possible that one impact of a free college program (note that the word "free" short-circuits decision-making processes for people, which is an issue I won't get into at this point) is to lead some students to choose a community college instead of a small college. But that impact can be overstated. After all, the community college was less expensive even before it was free, and every year the small college successfully recruited students. An economist will encourage people to make decisions based on net benefits—benefits minus costs—not based exclusively on the lowest cost. And a good admissions program will educate people on the ways that the higher cost for a small college pays off in demonstrable benefits for students who attend and graduate.

Arguing that the damage won't be catastrophic is a long way from arguing that the free college program is a good thing. To make that case, we need to move from analyzing the intensive margin to include the extensive margin. What?!

There are two types of people: those who intend to enroll in college and those who do not. Intensive margin analysis focuses on how those who intend to enroll distribute themselves among the available colleges. The intensive margin is where it is unambiguous that the impact of free college for a small college is negative. But that neglects the ways that a free college program can affect the extensive margin, the choice of people whether to attend college or not.

There are three ways that free community college helps small college enrollment. First, it encourages some people to attend community college who would not have attended college at all in the past. Remember my remark about "free"? For some students, community college tuition is already covered by state and federal government grants if they fill out and submit the Federal financial aid form (FAFSA). Putting the word "free" in the headline, along with related government policy to encourage completion of the FAFSA, is enough to help them realize the potential benefits of college attendance. Some of those students will succeed at the community college and decide to transfer to the small college. Transfer students are disproportionately successful at small colleges, so this will provide a further source of these high-quality members of the community.

A second way that free college helps is by reframing the college affordability question. There is a great deal of misleading media coverage on college affordability. A typical example cherry-picks a student who has accumulated an unrepresentative amount of debt in pursuit of an unrepresentative degree program that seems not to make financial sense ("Student Has $1M in Loans and a Degree in Petting Rabbits"). It happens, but it is not typical at small colleges. When students and families perceive that at least some types of college are affordable, then it opens the possibility of having a conversation about the net benefits of a small college. After all, if they aren't convinced, they always have free community college to fall back on. There is some evidence that one reason that free college is attractive is because it reduces the uncertainty about college tuition. As we will see in chapter 8, people are nervous about situations that involve uncertainty. College costs are not only substantial, but they are also typically not known until the student is well into the process. There are online financial aid calculators, but they are not necessarily accurate, and they are not universally used, in part because even a "simple" one can require a fair amount of work. Colleges who can't offer "free" might at least consider offering "certain" as a way to keep students engaged (Burland et al. 2023).

A third way that free college helps is more restricted to states that adopt it early. When I moved to Tennessee, some of my friends in other states were concerned about the overall educational environment. The best that could be said was, in a Tennessee leader's undiplomatic phrasing (I won't attribute it to protect the guilty), "At least we're not Mississippi." I suspect that people in Mississippi were saying the same thing about Tennessee. After the free college program was announced in 2014, the national narrative shifted to "Tennessee is a leader in creating innovative policies to help people invest in education." As a small college in Tennessee, that improved the overall picture of the state to which we recruited students, faculty, and staff.

What's the point? When analyzing a situation, don't only think about the people who are already involved. Remember the extensive margin and the way that people might join—or depart from—the situation based on whatever change you are making. As an exercise, think about alumni engagement from this perspective.

Exit, Voice, and Good-Old Boyalty: Understanding Alumni Engagement

Alumni are a major source of financial support for small colleges. Both as individuals and in their role influencing corporate and government donations, alumni can have a significant monetary impact on their alma mater. They also make enormous nonpecuniary contributions by donating their time to further college activities.

Perhaps the most fascinating aspect of alumni activity is that it is strictly voluntary. A standard paradigm for analyzing alumni contributions is as a delayed tuition payment. The idea is that people are aware that their tuition payments do not cover the full cost of their education, and so they make contributions to repay this debt. (Rice University made this point in the letter they sent when I was admitted to the school.) Another reason for contributions could be altruism, because people believe that their contributions can help others and that it's the right thing to do. Finally, there is a conspicuous consumption justification, in which people give in order to impress others.

One weakness of a simple financial analysis of alumni contributions is that it does not explain the substantial amount of volunteer time and other in-kind contributions. For leaders of small colleges looking to mobilize alumni support, both in financial and other terms, it would be helpful to understand why people give.

The most important fact about the relationship between an individual and an institution embodied in the term "alumnus" or "alumna" is that the relationship is prohibitively costly to exit. To put it simply, it's on the resume. Because potential employers (or just people you want to impress) associate the current perceived quality of the college one attended with one's ability, it is important that the college maintain or improve its quality and prestige. This is a motivation for alumni to be involved. Further, the inability to leave the relationship means that they should look for ways to be involved that maximize their impact on moving the institution in a way they think best.

There is a curious mechanism here. What is important is not the perceived quality of the college at the time the person attended—presumably the time that college had its biggest impact—but rather the perceived quality *today*. Graduating from a particular college is like purchasing a share of stock in a company and not being allowed to sell the stock. If the company does well, your share pays dividends; otherwise it doesn't. One necessity for a flourishing college is sound finances. The benefits that a graduate received and didn't pay for can be thought of as "accounts receivable" to the college. If the alumni don't pay them, the college is worse off, which in turn might lower the value of the degree. That is a simple economic explanation of why people might give, but it doesn't address why people might volunteer time as opposed to paying money.

Albert Hirschman (1970) developed a theory of the ways that people attempt to influence the behavior of organizations. He distinguished "exit" behavior, in which a person severs the relationship to influence the institution, with "voice" behavior, in which a person endeavors to influence the institution from within. The canonical example of exit behavior is the interaction between buyers and sellers underlying most economic analysis. If a buyer is dissatisfied with the product provided by a seller, then the buyer can leave and find another seller. A familiar example of voice is an election, where voters use their suffrage to install their preferred candidates in office and hope thereby to favorably affect government policy. Hirschman emphasizes that the choice by an individual whether to use exit or voice depends on the relative cost of the two options.

An important way that a person can increase the influence of their potential exit or their use of voice is to demonstrate loyalty to the institution. For example, if a person who has always shopped at a particular grocery store threatens to move their business, the management is more likely to react than if a casual customer makes the same threat. Similarly, before exercising voice in some institutions, there is a mandatory waiting or probationary period, as is the case in some exclusive clubs.

"No Exit"—The Relationship Between Alumni and Colleges

Let's now focus on the relationship between a person and the college from which they graduated. It is prohibitively costly to exit that relationship. I will always be a member of the Rice University class of 1985, whether or not I approve of Rice University's current or proposed policies. Given that exit is impossible, the only way for alumni to influence their alma mater is by using voice. (Alumni always have the option of exiting from the category of donors, whether in money or time, to the college.) Therefore, the key is to understand how alumni can use voice to influence decisions. As already noted, one way to maximize the impact of voice is to demonstrate loyalty.

The model I'm presenting implies that alumni act to maintain or increase the reputation of their college because this good reputation increases their own prospects and prestige. A familiar example would be spending time recruiting outstanding high schoolers to attend their college. Similarly, it includes the "old school ties" of alumni who assist the careers not only of friends but also strangers who happened to graduate from the same school. If one approximates the financial contribution of these in-kind gifts by the hourly wage of the people making them, it amounts to a substantial figure, although it is difficult to quantify the total across all institutions. Because financial donations are considered in many rankings, there is an added reason to donate to improve the school's prestige.

The question, then, is why a person might prefer one form of contribution over another. A possible explanation is that time contributions can be more precisely targeted to areas that the alumni think are most valuable. In addition, making a financial gift that captures the attention of the institution might be relatively more difficult for some people than making a gift of time, especially if that time is relatively pleasant. The boosters of an athletic club or cultural organization on campus get to enjoy fellowship and performances as well as try to influence the college.

Although the discussion to this point has separated contributions of time from contributions of money, they are often interrelated. As one alumna was quoted (Matthews, 1991), "Ask me for my ideas, my advice, my participation, as well as for my money. Make me part of an ongoing community. . . . my pocketbook would be wide open." These are welcome words to a college leader.

4

Portfolio

“Don’t put all your eggs in one basket.” This is advice that manages to be a cliché while simultaneously being misunderstood and ignored. The point of this advice is that it is difficult to know in advance which investments will be successful and which investments will not. Therefore, an investor should include multiple investments—diversify their portfolio—to reduce the chance of losing everything. That doesn’t sound so hard. But as is so often the case, there are some key issues that are necessary for successfully implementing this advice. Colleges that are one semester away from a crisis are in special need of avoiding disastrous outcomes, making it imperative for them to appropriately diversify.

The biggest misunderstanding is that simply increasing the number of investments is the same as diversifying the portfolio. Consider one of the most famous risky investments in literary history, Antonio’s ships pledged as collateral to Shylock in *The Merchant of Venice*. Suppose that I had invested in a cargo carried on one of the ships. Then my investment could be lost if the ship is sunk, captured by pirates, or otherwise prevented from delivering the cargo. Because of this risk, I cleverly think that I’ll diversify by investing in a second cargo. But if it is carried on the same ship, I haven’t altered my chances of losing everything. To truly diversify, I would need to invest in not only a different cargo but preferably a cargo that is more likely to be delivered in situations where my original cargo might not make it.

The technical term for this sort of diversification is finding investments that are negatively correlated with each other. The math can get as complicated as you want it to be, but the basic idea is that diversification comes from investments that are not successful at the same time (or unsuccessful at the same time). A homely example is betting on the outcome of a sporting event. My favorite Premier League team is Chelsea. If Chelsea plays, I want them to win. If they lose, I'll be unhappy. A way to reduce that unhappiness is to bet on their opponent to win. That way, if Chelsea wins the game, I'm happy even though I lose my bet, and if Chelsea loses the game, I'm unhappy with the result but I'm happy because I won some money. You can see why this is tricky advice. Who wants to bet against their favorite team?

Endowment

The most familiar context for discussing portfolio diversification is the college's endowment and related investment funds. These funds, while large compared to most people's assets, are nevertheless relatively small. A study by the National Association of College and University Business Officers (NACUBO), a national organization of chief financial officers, found that the average college endowment as of 2023 was $1.2 billion, with a median of $216 million.[1] This figure is skewed by the large endowments at a small number of schools—Harvard's was $49.4 billion, and "only" 142 schools, or 20 percent, were over $1 billion. The data are also misleading because only 699 colleges and universities participated, and it is likely that nonparticipation is more concentrated among schools with small endowments. For example, neither of the colleges where I was president are in the data, and

I can testify that their *combined* endowments are well below $216 million.

In part because of the rise of defined-contribution retirement accounts, there is a broad understanding of the importance of a diverse portfolio of investments. Nevertheless, small colleges regularly fall into some predictable bad habits.

One bad habit is trying to emulate the portfolio composition of prominent universities. Yale University famously pioneered the use of illiquid investments to increase the return on its endowment, which has led to a proliferation of college endowments purchasing real estate, private equity, and other assets that are not readily tradable. The person most responsible, David Swensen, described Yale's approach in his book published in 2000 (Swensen 2000). This was plausible for small schools to copy when it seemed to offer countercyclical stability, but in practice it generates market return at best with much higher fees. What's the problem? There are two. The first problem is scale, which in turn has implications for returns. Yale (and other famous examples) can invest large amounts, which implies that they are sought-after partners and that they also can pay for top-quality advice. Harvard pays its investment managers over $38 million annually (Rosenberg 2024), while a small college might have a total endowment of only $38 million. The NACUBO study found that 74 of the 699 schools that voluntarily reported their endowments were less than $38 million. By comparison, the 74th largest endowment was just over $2 billion. Suppose, for example, that a fund has a minimum investment of $50 million and a college's endowment is only $40 million. In that case, it will not be able to participate. The second problem is that Yale and its peers are better positioned to take on the risk of not being able to liquidate part of their portfolio. Most small colleges rely on their endowment draws to help cover basic operating costs, including financial aid, so that reducing liquidity can have an immediate impact on (already strained) operating budgets.

The second bad habit is adjusting portfolios based on looking backward at returns rather than forward at expected returns. A common refrain among college trustees is that because some class of investment was very successful last year, more of the endowment should be invested there. Because those sorts of relative returns are not persistent, following such a strategy would typically mean buying high and selling low—the antithesis of the formula for making money in the market.

A third bad habit, which is similar to looking backwards to choose winners, is trying to time purchases and sales to maximize returns rather than remaining invested in an appropriate portfolio. A charitable view is that market timers are trying to repeat the experience of Joseph in Egypt, who successfully interpreted Pharaoh's dream as guidance to save during the seven fat years in order to build up reserves to survive the seven lean years (Genesis 41:28–36). But unless you're getting the tip directly from God, market timing is unlikely to work. And being a little bit off on market timing matters a lot. There are many studies documenting returns that are highly concentrated in time yet hard to predict. For example, a 2024 report from J. P. Morgan Asset Management (47) found that investing in the S&P 500 index yielded 9.7 percent per year between January 2004 and December 2023. However, that return dropped to 5.5 percent if the investor was not invested on the ten best days and to 2.8 percent if the investor missed the twenty best days. To make things more difficult, six of the seven best days occurred after the worst days, and seven of the ten best days occurred within two weeks of the ten worst days. If you missed the forty best days—in a twenty-year period, remember—the return was −1.2 percent, so the investor would have lost money.

A more natural and cost-effective way of building a diversified portfolio is by using index funds and other passive investments. They have a low cost, provide the stability of diverse investments, and enable the college to get rich slowly, a much more desirable outcome than trying unsuccessfully to get rich quickly.

Enrollment Diversification

For small colleges, the opportunities for portfolio diversification that are both most lucrative and most challenging involve enrollment. After all, that's where the bulk of their revenues come from. And, unlike the case with endowments, there is not a standard tool like an index fund to purchase off the shelf as a baseline.

Geography

Most small colleges recruit from a limited geography. While individual studies vary, a common finding is that the overwhelming majority of students travel less than five hours away from home to attend school. This figure hasn't changed in decades, except perhaps to decrease, ironically enough, in the age of ubiquitous communication provided by smartphones. This means that a school is captive to the demographics of its surrounding area, which can be challenging for campuses located in areas with declining populations. Given that schools can't move their main campus (or at least not easily), how is it possible to geographically diversify their student body?

One form of geographic diversification is to recruit students from areas that are growing. For example, a school in New England can try to attract students from Texas or Florida. However, this effort tends to be futile because of the limited distance that most students are willing to travel. Unless there is a strong reason for a student to travel more than five hours, they probably won't. One way of framing this issue is that students must drive past many small colleges on the way to yours—why would they pass them by?

So if students need a reason to attend, then colleges that want to geographically diversify their student body need to be distinctive. An important driver of enrollment at small colleges is athletics, because the opportunity to continue competing at the intercollegiate level is attractive to many people. Athletics can also serve as an important geographic diversifier. For example, during my time at Columbia College, a significant portion of our students from outside South Carolina were recruited athletes. In the Southeast, in addition to the basic geographic inertia, most states deploy lottery-funded scholarships restricted to students who attend public or private colleges within their home state. The prospect of intercollegiate athletics can be a reason for students and their families to forego those home-state funds. Sometimes, there is the side benefit of attracting students who are relatively wealthier, which not only reduces strain on need-based financial aid but is correlated with retention beyond the first year and ultimately graduation.

Another potential source of diversification is to expand recruitment within the existing geographic region to high schools that have been underrepresented at the school. For example, when I was at Maryville College, there was a growing population of homeschooled students and graduates of private religious high schools in our core recruiting area. These students had historically gravitated to schools with a stricter Christian orientation than Maryville, but their growing numbers presented an opportunity to attract some who found our approach a better fit. For this type of outreach to truly represent diversification, enrollment of these students would need to be negatively correlated to enrollment of students from public schools in the same geography. While I didn't observe enough data to confirm or reject this possibility, it is not one that can be dismissed out of hand.

The advent of online education—and its ubiquity as an emergency response during the pandemic—would seem to provide a way to recruit with no geographic restrictions. In reality, it's not that simple. First, among traditional-age (18–22) college students, there remains a strong pull of campus life. For those students, online courses are a supplement to their residential experience, not a substitute for it. Second, most schools do not possess a strong enough brand to attract a student beyond their home region when competing with national giants like Southern New Hampshire University or Western Governors University. The exceptions tend to be specific programs within schools. At Columbia College, we signed articulation agreements with community colleges in South Dakota and Wyoming for our undergraduate speech language pathology program, which was strong and which no college in those states offered. But most of our online students came from the same restricted radius around Columbia, South Carolina, from which we drew residential students.

Academic Programs

The mention of online programs takes us from geography to another broad dimension of diversification: the type of academic program. At Columbia College, for example, we provided both undergraduate and graduate programs and delivered them in residential and online forms, both during the day and the evening. This variety of programs and modes of delivery provided useful diversification during the COVID pandemic. The traditional undergraduate program (residential, daytime, targeted to 18- to 22-year-olds) lost over 20 percent of its enrollment from 2019 to 2020, and despite growing, had not recovered to its prepandemic level when I departed in 2023. Despite that sobering issue, we increased our total enrollment by about 25 percent during that same period. How? It was through online and graduate programs. In addition, we began enrolling men in the traditional undergraduate program in 2020 and allowed them to live on campus and added men's athletic teams in 2021. Because of changing demand for single-gender education, the trajectory of the traditional program had been downward for many years before 2020.

The poor performance of the traditional undergraduate program relative to the online and graduate programs during the pandemic illustrates an important and often misunderstood element of a diverse portfolio. A negative correlation in performance precisely means that during times that one program is up, another program should be down. Well-intentioned efforts to ensure financial viability and stability often lead to such crude tools as a required "profit" margin every year for every program. (The issue of a nonprofit college earning a profit will be explored at length in chapter 5.) This is unwise for the obvious reason that the program that is struggling this year might be the one that provides you with the revenue and students you need in a few years when today's successful program is struggling. This is the essence of diversification.

There is a more subtle issue here too. Often, academic programs are compared in terms of the revenue they generate relative to the costs of educating the students enrolled in them. At York College of Pennsylvania, we calculated a revenue–cost ratio for every academic program. This was intended as a useful heuristic rather than a definitive tool, as it simply took the pro-rated tuition revenue from students enrolled in courses in the program and compared it to the salaries of instructors in the program. (No capital costs were included, among other omissions.) When I tell people about this exercise and ask them to guess which programs were highly rated, they often guess programs like business, engineering, and nursing that are publicly celebrated for launching students to well-paying careers. Wrong. The most lucrative programs were the humanities, which taught every student in general education courses and whose faculty were relatively less expensive than engineers, accountants, and nurses. (This is one explanation for why community colleges advocate for public support based on technical education but rely so heavily on providing general education courses to subsidize those other programs.) In fact, typically, nursing had costs that exceeded revenues, as small clinical course sizes required by both our clinical partners and the accreditor failed to provide enough revenue to cover the salaries of nursing professors. And recall, this measure doesn't include expensive hardware, such as simulators, involved in nursing.

So why offer nursing if it doesn't even cover its costs? Interestingly, it comes back to the question of intensive versus extensive margins that we discussed in chapter 3. The revenue–cost ratio took as a given that a certain number of students had enrolled in the college. This is an intensive margin analysis, which neglects the question of why those students enrolled in the first place. Most of the students in the general education courses had not chosen to enroll at York in order to take them, no matter how disappointing that fact might be to the faculty in those disciplines. (Full disclosure: I've been one of them, regularly teaching principles of microeconomics to students who did not enroll in college because of the chance to learn economics.) What nursing provides is a halo effect, in which students and their families see a thriving program in this rigorous and relevant area as evidence of the overall quality of the school. Engineering can play much the same role. Further, by attracting employers for these in-demand fields, it creates opportunities for students throughout the school to successfully start their careers, which in turn provides a boost to recruitment efforts as the school can demonstrate positive outcomes for its graduates.

A final dimension of diversity that has been the topic of increased public scrutiny is the political and academic perspectives of the faculty and staff. If the faculty and staff are homogeneous, then there is a risk of being unable to attract students if their (or their family's) worldview is incompatible with that of the campus. The growing attention to free speech and constructive disagreement on campus is welcome in that sense, and schools that are able to credibly represent themselves as intellectually and politically diverse are likely to be more robust than those that are a monoculture. The idea of diversification is both simple and complicated, and it resonates throughout the operation of a college in nonobvious ways.

A Challenge in Diversifying

When we consider diversity, we are subdividing the entire population into groups. If these groups are defined so that each person belongs to one group, then adding up the groups will equal the entire population. This might seem like a trivial observation, but this adding-up constraint or accounting identity has some implications for those working to diversify their campus.[2]

Consider a simple case of two groups: purple students and garnet students. Suppose that there are 1,200 students enrolled at the college, with 300 purple and 900 garnet. Further suppose that all students live on campus. No matter how you split the students up, on average, each residence hall (or floor) will have a student body that is 25 percent purple and 75 percent garnet. For example, if one residence hall is 50 percent purple, then it must be the case that another residence hall is less than 25 percent purple.

Perhaps that doesn't sound too complicated. But now consider a smaller scale view of diversity. Suppose that the campus residence halls consist of four-person suites. Let us also assume that purple students would like to live with garnet students to broaden their experiences, and similarly for garnet students. Finally, let us suppose that neither student wants to be in the minority in their own suite. These reasonable conditions imply that the only stable housing arrangement is one in which 50 percent of the residence suites are entirely occupied by garnet students, while the other 50 percent are occupied by two garnet students and two purple students each. If a garnet student is assigned to a suite with three purple students, they will want to move out because they are a minority. The same is true for a purple student assigned to live with three garnet students.

Thus, a relatively benign set of circumstances, in which every student wants to live in a diverse environment, results in an outcome in which half of the student body is living in a nondiverse suite. And it could be worse. Consider the following small change in preferences, in which each purple and garnet student prefers to live with students of the opposite color but wants to be in the majority in their suite. In that case, the only stable outcome is complete segregation.

The moral of the story is that diversification is tricky, even when people are well-intentioned. Another moral is that it is important to look beyond both averages and extreme cases when trying to understand a situation. Return to the situation from two paragraphs ago, where half of the suites are integrated and half are segregated. Can we infer that the garnet students living with only garnet students are prejudiced against purple? We cannot, because we already specified what everyone's preferences were. In reality, of course, we aren't provided with everyone's preferences. But even this simple example is a reason to pause before ascribing bad motivations to explain an outcome that isn't desired.

Let's consider one other complication before we move on. Suppose that the trustees have decided that the college should be equally represented by purple and garnet students, and suppose they want the change to happen in one year. To keep things simple, let's suppose that each class has 300 students—75 purple and 225 garnet—and that every student graduates in four years and every student returns every year. (Ah, if only student retention and graduation were that simple.) In that case, after the seniors graduate, we are left with 900 students: 225 purple and 675 garnet. To meet the requirements of the trustees, we would need to enroll 600 purple and 600 garnet in the next year. That is impossible. The closest we could come is to enroll a first-year class of 300 purple students and zero garnet students, moving the total student population to 525 purple and 675 garnet. Now, it would be straightforward to meet the trustees' requirement in four years, just by enrolling new classes evenly divided between purple and garnet. The lesson is that if we want to make change happen quickly, we must move beyond the desired distribution. That might or might not be financially, educationally, or politically feasible. (For an exercise, consider what to do if there are only 125 potential purple students each year.)

The heterogeneity of American higher education among both the types of institutions and the students represented is perhaps its greatest strength. The point of the illustrations here is not to argue against work to add diversity in multiple dimensions but to encourage clear thinking about some of what Schelling (1978, 45) calls "the inescapable mathematics of musical chairs."

5

Making a Profit

Private colleges in the United States are typically organized as nonprofit institutions. The word "nonprofit" is often misconstrued as implying that the institution is required to operate at a loss. A moment's reflection should be enough to realize that such a situation would not be stable, as eventually the losses would add up and require the college to close. The nonprofit identity refers to a legal constraint that any operating surplus or profit be reinvested to advance the mission of the organization. In order to thrive, a college must earn a profit or, more precisely, enjoy total revenues that exceed its total costs.

To an economist, a college is an example of a company. While basic economic analysis assumes that companies are trying to maximize profit, this analysis can readily be adapted to the more complex situation of a college trying to maximize its impact based on its mission. Even in this more complex case, it is important to keep track of profit and make sure it is positive (or at least non-negative). No matter how effectively a college advances its mission, if it consistently operates at a loss, it will eventually go out of business.

Profits are equal to total revenues minus total costs. For a small college, the bulk of revenue will be directly related to student enrollment. These revenues include tuition, fees, room, board, and sometimes other auxiliary operations such as bookstores or parking. Other important revenue sources include philanthropic gifts, government grants, and a wide range of nonacademic activities that vary substantially from place to place. At Maryville College, for example, there was an extremely active set of summer camps that generated substantial revenue. I know of at least one small college (Bethany College in West Virginia) that received mineral rights royalties from fracking on land it owned.

The largest cost for small colleges is payroll, including both salary and benefits. Most colleges also have a substantial physical plant to care for, along with the costs of acquiring and maintaining technology. There are also costs for academic materials such as laboratory supplies and books, costs for services such as travel for professional development or for athletic teams, and nonacademic costs such as debt service or legal fees.

A cost that is real but often neglected is the ongoing depreciation of physical assets. Because the campus buildings don't submit a bill every year for needed repairs or maintenance, a school that is operating on a narrow margin can be tempted to delay taking care of the buildings. This "deferred maintenance" is a common phenomenon that causes the true financial condition of a college to be worse than its apparent situation based on cash inflows and outflows. Another subtle form of deferred maintenance is the neglect of funding professional development for faculty and staff, which can lead to people not being as effective as possible. Even worse is not increasing compensation over time, which can lead to the loss of people who are most effective and have the most outside options. (We will return to the issue of deferred maintenance in chapter 6 and to the impact of deferred maintenance in professional development and compensation on faculty and staff in chapter 7.)

So a college needs to earn a profit, even if it is not trying to maximize profit and even though it is constrained to reinvest that profit. How does a company earn a profit? We have already seen that economists like to focus on activities at the margin—in other words what happens when small changes are made. This idea shows up here in comparing the marginal revenue of an activity with its marginal cost. For example, enrolling one more student generates revenue from tuition and other sources, and the marginal revenue is the amount of tuition the additional student adds to the revenue received from the previous students who were already enrolled. Similarly, the marginal cost from a student is the incremental increase in costs that results from adding that student to the college. For profit to increase, the marginal revenue must exceed the marginal cost.

Some otherwise puzzling behavior by colleges becomes clearer if one identifies the marginal cost and marginal revenue generated by the behavior in question. For example, the ongoing escalation in tuition discounting, regularly decried by insiders and outside observers alike, is easy to understand when the marginal costs and marginal revenues are compared. Likewise, the focus on retaining students is not only generated by the desire to help them graduate and succeed but also from the impact on marginal costs and marginal revenues. This reasoning highlights the potential peril of situations in which it is difficult to make small changes, whether for structural, contractual, or political reasons.

Price Discrimination

An important technical concept in economic analysis is price discrimination. To an economist, "discrimination" means treating people differently based on one or more of their observable characteristics. A familiar example is purchasing an airline ticket. You pay a different price depending on whether you purchase in advance or on the day of the flight, even though you are receiving the same service of being transported from one place to another. In addition, you might have to pay more to have an improved level of service, whether that be a more comfortable seat, the opportunity to board early and use scarce overhead storage space, or any other amenity that the airline thinks you might be willing to pay for.

Why do companies charge different prices? The short answer is that different people are willing to pay different amounts for the same service. From the company's point of view, what would be best is if each person would pay the maximum amount they're willing to pay. There are a couple of challenges in achieving that outcome, though. People are unlikely to honestly reveal the maximum amount, even if they are aware of it. After all, customers would prefer to receive a good or service for the lowest possible price. Therefore, a company must make inferences about how much someone will pay. Returning to the airline ticket example: someone booking in advance might have more flexibility in travel than someone booking the day of the flight, so the advance purchaser is willing to pay less for a given flight. Identifying which category someone is in is not free, so charging multiple prices costs more than charging one price.

Even if a company can figure out how much someone is willing to pay, it needs to be able to prevent someone from circumventing its approach. If I wanted to make some money, I could buy a ticket in advance for a low price and sell it to someone who wanted to travel on short notice for a high price. As long as I charge less than the airline, the purchaser thinks it is a good deal. Therefore, companies that charge different prices need to make sure that it is difficult, or ideally impossible, for someone to engage in buying at a low price and reselling at a higher price. Anticipating the discussion about regulatory capture in chapter 10, note that it is in the airlines' interest to forbid the resale of tickets. Thus, they will favor measures such as requiring the passenger's name on the ticket and showing identification to confirm it, regardless of whether there are any benefits in terms of enhanced security.

If it's difficult and costly to charge different prices, why do it? The benefit to the company is the possibility of charging high enough prices to people who are willing to pay more that the additional revenues exceed the costs of identifying them. Conversely, there can be benefits of charging a low price if a good or service is going to expire or if there is a very low marginal cost of providing it. An empty seat on a flight cannot be sold the following day, so the marginal revenue can exceed the marginal cost for that seat even at a very low price.

Tuition Discounting

The metaphor of selling airline tickets translates with perhaps disturbing ease to the case of charging students to attend college. Each person is willing to pay a different amount, so colleges potentially lose money by charging less than some people are willing to pay. But any empty spots in a particular semester are gone for good, so colleges potentially lose money by charging a price such that not enough people enroll. A way for colleges to make as much net revenue as possible from enrollment is to charge a variety of prices. This practice is known as tuition discounting, and it is nearly universally practiced, especially among nonelite institutions. In fact, at many institutions, more than 90 percent of students pay less than the published tuition (or "sticker price" in college administrator jargon). Not only are a large number of students affected, but the extent of discounting is substantial. The average discount has steadily increased over the past few decades, and it is now about 50 percent. In other words, on average, a student will only pay half of the listed tuition price.

There are three main ways that price discrimination is implemented. The first approach is through so-called need-based aid. The idea here is that people with fewer financial resources will be charged less. Or, to put it differently, people with more financial resources will be charged more. The second approach is differential tuition for higher-cost programs, especially those in high demand because they are viewed as leading to higher-paying professions. Examples include nursing and engineering, while some schools achieve the same effect through course fees tied to lab courses or other courses that are expensive to deliver. The third approach is through so-called merit aid. The idea here is that people who bring special skills or who will enhance the college experience for others will be charged less. This is a way of bringing in talented section leaders for music programs, athletes to entertain and inspire the community, or scholars who will raise the academic profile of the school. In practice, at many places, this merit-based aid is an entitlement based on possessing the characteristics required to be admitted. In other words, it is a psychological ploy. In addition, if the entering student population is relatively needy (not wealthy), then the merit aid is simultaneously a relabeled need-based aid.

There is an entire industry devoted to helping colleges maximize net tuition revenue (tuition paid after financial aid is subtracted). Elaborate statistical models are deployed to help determine what level of aid is needed to persuade the desired quantity of students with the desired characteristics to enroll.[1]

One idea that emerges from economic theory is that people who have many choices (technically, a higher price elasticity of demand) can command a higher discount than people with few choices (lower price elasticity of demand). In higher education terms, people with many choices are those who are desirable to many colleges. Among the most desirable characteristics are high academic ability (as illustrated through high grades, advanced placement tests, or high standardized test scores) and high family income (both to pay for current costs and perhaps for future philanthropic contributions). Because measured academic ability, particularly test scores and advanced placement, are correlated with family income and wealth, the result is that tuition discounting can result in students from wealthier households paying less than students from poorer households. (Phil Levine has documented this issue using data on selective private colleges in his 2022 book.)

A reasonable question to ask is why colleges post such a high tuition price if they know they are only going to get paid 50 percent of it. I was regularly asked this question during board meetings at Maryville College, which had a high discount rate. Wouldn't it be easier just to cut the posted tuition in half? Easier, perhaps, but not optimal for generating the revenue to pursue its mission. By cutting the price, it would reduce the opportunity to charge a higher price to people who are willing to pay more. Granted, there may only be a few of them, but every dollar counts.

Another reason to list a high price and then discount is a familiar phenomenon known as the "Chivas Regal effect," in which a high price is assumed to reflect high quality. A school that charges substantially lower tuition than its peers is immediately suspected of providing a lower quality experience, even if the net tuition (after discounting) is identical to its peers. During my time there, York College of Pennsylvania was an example of a school that charged low tuition, provided high-quality education, and was forced to spend a great deal of time justifying itself.

A final reason to engage in discounting from a high starting price is an idea in behavioral economics of a reference point that people use to determine their satisfaction with a situation. Anything that is an improvement over the reference point is considered good, while anything worse than the reference point is bad. The published tuition for a college is the reference point for families considering attending the school. Mathematically, there is no difference between charging $30,000 tuition with a $10,000 discount and charging $20,000 tuition. But extensive psychological and economic research shows that people prefer the first situation over the second one because of the change in reference point. In nontechnical terms, people like to think they're getting a bargain because the price they pay is less than the published price. In addition, there are the bragging rights that my child earned a $10,000 scholarship. Some colleges, when sending a letter offering the financial aid package, multiply the annual scholarship by 4 to help the parents brag even more.

Retention

At most small colleges, only about half of the students who arrive directly from high school graduate from the college in four years.

Sometimes students discover that their needs are better served elsewhere, so they transfer and are successful. This mobility to find the best fit is a very positive feature of the American higher education system. Too often, though, students depart without achieving a meaningful academic credential, which can leave them worse off than their counterparts who didn't attend college at all, due to the lost opportunity to earn wages combined with the accumulation of debt. Colleges therefore have a moral imperative to help students persist and succeed. Beyond this moral imperative, there is also a financial imperative based on marginal revenues and marginal costs.

It is very expensive to recruit a new student. These expenses include purchasing names of prospective students, communicating with them electronically and through print, and employing admissions counselors (recruiters) to inform students about the advantages of their college and persuade students to enroll. Because there are so many students and so many colleges, a great deal of this effort is wasted in the sense that it is devoted to students who will not enroll in your college.

Retaining students, by contrast, is relatively straightforward. If we think of retention as "recruiting sophomores," then the idea is clear. Every student we are recruiting is not only known to us but has already demonstrated a willingness to enroll in (and perhaps relocate to) our college. This means that every dollar devoted to their success addresses a student who is enrolled at our college. The marginal cost of recruiting a sophomore is much less than the marginal cost of recruiting a new student.

Because most schools have relatively stable pricing and financial aid (price discrimination) approaches, the marginal revenue (net tuition revenue) per student won't change much from year to year. Therefore, the surplus (marginal revenue minus marginal cost) from retaining a student is substantially higher than the surplus from recruiting a new student.

This increased surplus from retained students can help explain an otherwise confusing aspect of college pricing, which is the fact that some high-income students pay a lower net tuition than low-income students. As we already noted, a standard dimension of price discrimination is based on measured academic performance, which is positively correlated with the wealth and educational background of the student's family. Why would a college direct money to a wealthier student? If that student is more likely to stay for four years and graduate, then the net tuition revenue the college can expect to receive will be larger than what the college can expect from a student who is statistically likely not to stay for four years. While there are also reasons based on academic rankings and faculty preferences, it would be a mistake to overlook this fundamental financial reason for preferring students from wealthy and well-educated families, not to mention the potential for philanthropic gifts both during their time on campus and in the future.

One of the challenges for colleges is that students affect each other's performance. This can be negative, as in the case of a student who has decided to drop out but remains living on campus and creates a nuisance that distracts other students. Or it can be positive, as in the case of a student who encourages others to perform at a high level. An intriguing finding from 2022 by Raj Chetty and coauthors is that students who make friends with wealthier students are themselves more likely to improve their social and economic standing. This complicates the picture, as now subsidizing the attendance of wealthier students can convey a social benefit on their classmates from less-wealthy backgrounds. Students don't necessarily take this impact into account when making their decisions, and economic theory generally encourages the subsidizing of decisions that have positive spillover effects.

Cross-Subsidies

So far, we have focused on the simple case of comparing the revenue from each student with the cost of educating them. In practice, though, there can be opportunities to use a surplus from one student, program, or activity to offset a deficit elsewhere. The requirement is that the college runs a surplus when all its activities are taken into account, not that every activity runs a surplus. The use of a surplus in one area to offset a deficit elsewhere is known as cross-subsidization.

One familiar cross-subsidizing policy is the requirement for students to live on campus for some of or all their time enrolled at a college. Wait a minute: I hear you say, isn't that requirement based on the importance of peer interaction and extracurricular learning in the full development of the student? And yes, there are benefits from bringing students together in this way. But neglecting the net revenue implications is to misunderstand the financial picture for colleges.

Most colleges own and operate considerable residential structures. If they were constructed or renovated using debt, there are principal and interest payments due every year. There are also utilities, such as water, sewer, electricity, and internet. Typically, there are also paid staff, both full-time and part-time (including student resident assistants). Almost all these costs are fixed. In other words, the costs don't change regardless of how many students live there. In addition, the total costs are usually a small fraction of the potential total revenue from housing students. Even if the college charges a rental price slightly below the market rate in the surrounding area, it has the advantage when compared to other landlords of borrowing at a tax-free interest rate and not owing property taxes.

By this point, you already know that it is especially important to compare the marginal cost and marginal revenue from a student living on campus. If the overall costs of operating a residence hall are fixed, then the marginal cost of an additional student is approximately zero. Thus, the entire marginal revenue from adding a student is surplus.

Allowing a room to be empty, then, means forgoing considerable net revenue. And this revenue can be used to help operate other parts of the college, without increasing tuition or other visible charges for students. The net revenue generated from a residential student is not simply the tuition and fees minus the cost of education; it is the tuition, fees, room, and board minus the cost of education, housing, and food. Running a substantial surplus on room and board means that colleges can invest more heavily in education at a given level of net tuition. Framing this important financial move as one focused on student development (which, again, is not entirely false) makes it more palatable, particularly given that financial aid can be used to price-discriminate on room and board too.

Another cross-subsidy is from academic programs that are low-cost to academic programs that are high-cost, as discussed in chapter 4. The low-cost areas tend to be programs with a surplus of available teachers that require little in terms of equipment. General education in such fields as English composition and literature, history, and political science are good examples. High-cost fields include engineering and nursing, which require hiring faculty who have lucrative professional opportunities outside of academia and considerable capital expenditure. Although the focus of this book is on four-year private colleges, this academic program cross-subsidy is perhaps most easily seen in the case of community colleges, which generate considerable public support based on (expensive) vocational education programs but then pay for those programs through the surplus generated by providing low-cost general education programs.

Personnel as a Quasi-Fixed Cost

When comparing marginal revenues and marginal costs, an important first step is to understand which costs are fixed and which are variable. The largest category of expenditures for most small colleges (outside of institutional financial aid) is payroll and benefits. Typically, about half of the total expenditures net of financial aid go to paying faculty and staff. Are these payments fixed or variable costs?

The definition of a fixed cost is that it doesn't change as the amount of output changes. Consider increasing enrollment by one student. It is unlikely that another professor or additional staff will need to be hired. If enrollment increases by enough, it will likely require additional people, but at least over some range, it makes sense to think of personnel costs as fixed.

Less obviously, it can be the case that colleges are reluctant to reduce employment as enrollment decreases. One reason for this reluctance is that there are substantial resource costs in recruiting and onboarding new people. This means it could be logical to keep "extra" personnel on hand during the downturn to have them available without the costs of recruiting them when enrollment increases again.

Another reason that some labor costs can be fixed even when enrollment declines is that some administrative functions are necessary regardless of the size of the school. For example, every college needs a registrar.

The reluctance to reduce the number of faculty is sometimes attributed to tenure. This is a misunderstanding of the legal nature of tenure, which is not, as commonly assumed, guaranteed lifetime employment. Rather, it simply requires a particular type of due process (which varies from school to school) before terminating the employment of a tenured professor. Typical reasons for termination include institutional financial distress, elimination of the academic program in which the professor is tenured, and poor performance by the professor. In practice, a college will incur considerable internal opprobrium and external criticism if it eliminates tenured positions, reinforcing the quasi-fixed nature of faculty costs when enrollment declines.

A final reason for employment not to vary much when enrollment declines is the impact on morale. As we will explore further in chapter 7, the people who choose to work in small colleges tend to differ in important ways from the people who work in other industries. As a result, nonpecuniary compensation plays a larger role in higher education, so maintaining morale is vital to operating productively and effectively. I know from personal experience that people will offer to take across-the-board pay cuts (to pay that is already relatively low) in order to avert layoffs or job cuts.

Enrollment declines can even be somewhat pleasant for some faculty and staff, who enjoy smaller workloads without any decrease in pay, at least for a while. That dynamic in turn exacerbates the negative morale impacts whenever a change is needed.

All the reasons outlined imply that colleges might not be quick to add positions when enrollment increases and will hesitate to reduce employment when enrollment decreases. This means that, for a range of enrollment, it is best to approximate labor costs as fixed rather than variable so that the marginal labor cost is about zero for that range.

An effective institutional leader can use this insight to help build net revenue by extending it to the level of academic programs. Essentially, any program not operating at full capacity is an opportunity to build surplus by adding enrollment. The additional students bring additional revenue without requiring additional faculty to be hired. At both the program and institutional level, this idea is one explanation for continued increases in tuition discounting. Even at a high discount rate, there is some additional revenue from enrolling a new student, while there is no additional cost. Those who propose to do away with tuition discounting need to find a way to eliminate this incentive. I believe it unlikely that they will be able to do so.

The other big implication of this analysis is that hiring (or downsizing) will typically not occur in incremental ways but in relatively large chunks. Essentially, if a college is going to deal with all the costs of changing the number of employees, it needs a substantial reason to do so. Further, it implies that a college facing enrollment declines is unlikely to gradually adjust to them. Rather, it will go on for a while before it is too painful to continue. An extreme example is the case of Sweet Briar College. When, in 2015, the college announced it was closing after years of declining enrollments,

I discovered that they employed almost exactly the same number of faculty and staff as Maryville College, where I was president. Maryville's enrollment was about double that of Sweet Briar's.[2] It seemed plausible to me that there might have been some incremental moves that Sweet Briar could have taken before the extreme step of closing the college. After all, when I became president of Maryville College in 2010, we faced a deficit stemming from the enrollment declines associated with the Great Recession. I ended up cutting several programs and positions, including some positions held by tenured faculty. While these moves made it possible for us to invest in the programs and people who remained, they did not endear me to the community, illustrating the challenge facing college leaders when enrollment declines.

6

One Semester Away from a Crisis

One fall semester we announced record enrollment figures for Maryville College. A few days later, a community friend asked me what I was worried about now, given that good news. I replied that my main worry was enrollment for the spring semester. They were surprised and asked when I would stop worrying about enrollment. My answer: when I was no longer president.

If the students don't show up, then the most important revenue source is absent (not to mention a lack of critical mass enabling academic and co-curricular activities to function at a high level). Even the healthiest small college is one semester away from a crisis.

When I teach principles of economics, I often say that all economics can be boiled down to two sentences: "People are trying to make themselves as happy as possible. Nothing is free." Everything else is just a matter of developing the implications of those two sentences.

One implication of those two sentences is that there are basically only two ways that a person can make themselves happier. First, they can acquire additional resources. Second, they can do a better job with their existing resources. The first approach can be described as one of abundance or, more technically, of focusing on the objective function. In other words, we are obtaining additional resources and using them in a way that makes us the happiest. The second approach is one of limits or, more technically, of focusing on the constraints. Our resources are limited, and we are considering whether their current use is best or whether they can be reallocated to make us happier.

An axiom of economics is that resources are scarce compared to what people desire. Hence, there is always the requirement to make choices, and there are always constraints on activity. In that sense, it makes no sense to distinguish between decisions necessitated by constraints and decisions taken to maximize the institution's impact or other desirable outcomes. In another sense, though, there are important insights to be gained by focusing on the nature of the limits that small colleges face, as these limits help explain some decisions that otherwise seem puzzling. It is especially helpful in explaining what seem like short-sighted decisions by colleges, as there is a natural correlation between the planning horizon and the abundance of resources.

Constraints on Small Colleges

Given that economists assume that every person and institution is constrained, it is not surprising that small colleges are constrained. What is most relevant for our purposes, though, are the ways in which the constraints on these schools are different from those facing other institutions.

One important constraint on small colleges is implicit in their name—they are small. This matters in a variety of ways, including economies of scale in purchasing and operating, but is especially relevant when it comes to regulation. As we will examine further in chapter 10, higher education is a very regulated industry. Often, regulation involves completing forms that are identical regardless of the size of the school. Simply put, there is a fixed cost of regulation. For example, every school whose students receive Federal financial aid must submit a form demonstrating its compliance with Federal regulations governing the distribution of the aid. In a large university, this fixed cost is relatively small compared to the overall cost of operations. In a small institution, it is a larger percentage of total cost.

The example of complying with Federal aid rules seems relatively small, even reasonable. I don't disagree, although the basic point that a fixed regulatory cost weighs heavier on smaller schools still stands. What is more vexing, though, is the case of more complicated regulatory issues. The one that has the biggest impact is Title IX. There are two fundamental problems with Title IX that complicate its important role in providing equitable access to education for every person. The first problem is that the regulatory structure implicitly assumes that a college employs at least one full-time attorney and that the college can easily add people to investigate accusations. The second problem is that the entire set of regulations is not stable, with fundamental changes in philosophy and implementation resulting from each change in presidential administration. The only thing worse than a large regulatory burden is a large regulatory burden that changes in unpredictable ways every few years.

Beyond regulation, which is an externally imposed constraint, there are also internally generated constraints. Enrollment-driven colleges face liquidity and capital restrictions by definition (otherwise they're not truly enrollment-driven). Most small colleges have borrowed as much money as their creditors will allow them to. This means they have limited ability to tap credit markets to weather short-term challenges or to invest in emergent long-run opportunities. Beyond this limit on borrowing, many (most) small colleges also have limited liquidity. For example, people often think that a college can spend its endowment on whatever it wants whenever it wants. In practice, there are strict legal constraints on the use of endowment funds, so even a school that has a robust endowment might in fact be extremely limited in the extent to which it has cash to quickly deploy.

Another example of a key constraint is the geographic location of the campus. (Of course, this can also be a key asset.) Even in a world of growing online instruction and remote work, there are substantial activities that rely on physical presence. A large university is a city unto itself. The year I spent as a visiting professor at the University of Michigan, it enrolled more than 50,000 students, which alone would qualify Ann Arbor as a metropolitan area. That year, I taught two sections of principles of microeconomics with a combined enrollment of more than 600 students. By contrast, Columbia College had about 600 students attending classes on campus in 2022—a group that could comfortably be assembled in just one classroom at its neighbor down the street, the University of South Carolina.

Small colleges do not create their surroundings, but they are strongly affected by them. A school in a remote rural area might be the largest employer in a substantial radius, but it won't be able to supply the amenities found in a metropolitan setting. A school located in a neighborhood that has seen better days is forced to spend resources on overcoming the negative perception of visitors. Naturally, colleges play a key role in promoting and maintaining the vibrancy of cities and regions, but they are not able to single-handedly change their surroundings.

Impact of Constraints on Planning Horizon

> Wowbagger the Infinitely Prolonged was—indeed, is—one of the Universe's very small number of immortal beings. . . . . To begin with it was fun; he had a ball, living dangerously, taking risks, cleaning up on high-yield long-term investments, and just generally outliving the hell out of everybody.
>
> —Douglas Adams, *Life, the Universe, and Everything*

If you are certain that you won't fail, it is not difficult to take risks. More broadly, the higher the cost of failure, the riskier an action can seem. A risk that for one person or institution seems small can be existential for another institution. Consider the impact of a needed car repair on a student who commutes to school. A student who has financial resources sufficient to cover the repair must deal with the costs in time and money of doing so. A student who lacks those resources might have to make difficult decisions that can include withdrawing from school.

A general rule of life is that everything looks easy to people who don't have to do it. Outside observers look at small colleges and make what they believe to be helpful suggestions. However, it is not always easy to implement those suggestions with the resources available.

For example, consider deferred maintenance, which is a euphemism for allowing the physical plant and other infrastructure to deteriorate. Why is there so much deferred maintenance at small colleges? Don't the leaders understand that it is much more efficient to have a well-structured plan for preventive maintenance that will maximize the useful life and minimize the long-run operating costs? In some cases, the answer is no. In other cases, it is because the leaders have a short-run horizon (all that matters is that it doesn't fall apart while I'm here) instead of the long-term horizon appropriate for a college. But even leaders who understand the situation and are motivated by the best interests of the college often defer maintenance. I was one of them. The reason is that cash flow today constrains their ability to invest in the long-term efficient maintenance of the physical plant. So not only is the quality less than it might otherwise be, but the overall cost for a given level of quality is high. As the cliché goes, "It's expensive to be poor."

The example of deferred maintenance is a specific instance of what an economist might see as a low-level equilibrium trap. That's a mouthful of jargon, so let me unpack it. An equilibrium is just a situation where no one has a reason to change. It's not necessarily desirable, and in fact much economic analysis of practical situations involves identifying ways to move from a less desirable equilibrium to a more desirable equilibrium.

The equilibrium for many small colleges is that they don't have sufficient resources to invest in their infrastructure, including the ongoing professional development and compensation of their faculty and staff. Because they can't invest, they aren't able to improve their performance to the extent that they can generate sufficient resources. As we saw in the model presented in chapter 1 and will develop further in chapter 11, colleges lack the ability to attract capital by offering investors a substantial financial return, so a college that wants to move out of the low-level equilibrium trap must find some other answer.

The economist's typical solution for a low-level equilibrium trap is called "the big push," which is exactly what it sounds like. The idea is to invest enough resources to reverse the negative dynamic of low resources leading to low performance leading to low resources. In a college setting, those resources typically need to come from public-sector investment or philanthropic investment. The major investments in historically Black colleges and universities since 2020 by the government both in the form of debt forgiveness and direct grants are a nice example of public-sector activity. The best example of philanthropy is set by Mackenzie Scott, who has provided promising institutions with substantial gifts and left the institutions free to invest them as they see fit.

Surrendering Surplus and Partnering with Loan Sharks

In chapter 5, we saw that providing housing is one of the crucial services that generate operating surplus for small colleges. Given that information, it might sound surprising that some colleges form partnerships with for-profit companies that provide housing for them. Why give up the surplus to an outside company?

The answer is that the college lacks the resources to invest in construction, operation, and maintenance of desirable housing. So, in an institutional version of the rent-to-own trap that low-income households can find themselves in, it allows an outside company to collect the surplus once the outside company invests in housing. Not only does the college surrender the surplus, but often it is required to guarantee a return on the investment of the outside company. This usually comes in the form of a required level of student occupancy, but sometimes it is an actual financial guarantee. How difficult can it be to require students to live in college-provided (even if not college-owned) property? The answer is not too difficult, provided that there are enough students enrolled. That's the catch. If enrollment falls, say because of a Great Recession or a COVID pandemic or just a bad year, then a resource-constrained college is even further on the hook. Small colleges didn't invent the problem of selling a major long-term asset for a small short-term gain. Genesis 25:29–34 tells the story of Esau selling his birthright in return for a bowl of soup—probably not the Biblical example that small colleges aspire to emulate.

Fortunately, not many colleges have taken such an extreme step in housing. However, there is a much more common example of this phenomenon when it comes to campus dining. Almost all colleges outsource dining services. A typical contract runs from five to ten years, and one component of the agreement is an investment from the company providing dining services. This investment is typically to upgrade the capital facilities used for dining, although sometimes it is directed elsewhere.

Who could be opposed to an investment in the college from a partner? The answer is no one, unless it turns out not to be what it seems at face value. The hidden part of the investment is that the college pays for it in installments over the course of the contract. For example, when I was president of Maryville College, we signed a ten-year contract with a food service provider. (Full disclosure: I'm a big fan of the company, despite what you might think after you read the next couple of sentences.) Part of the contract was an investment of about $2 million in improving the main campus dining facility. This investment was to be repaid over the contract period. Because the costs were itemized, we could figure out what the implicit interest rate was on the money. It was substantially higher than what the college was paying on its debt. So why not just borrow the money ourselves? We lacked borrowing capacity, and we also didn't have sufficient cash reserves to finance the improvements ourselves. So we paid a higher interest rate, without calling it that, to provide appealing services that attract students who provide revenue. It's extreme to call it loan sharking, but that's the basic logic of being able to charge above-market interest rates to credit-constrained institutions.

For colleges that outsource the maintenance of their physical plant, there are typically similar arrangements. I inherited such a situation at Columbia College, with a company that I'm not such a big fan of. But I won't dwell on the topic, because I suspect you've already gotten the point.

Risk Aversion and Constraints

I began my career by spending two decades at research institutions as a student and a professor. Until I joined a small college, I was unaware of the luxury I enjoyed at a research institution of being able to make choices knowing that those choices would not substantially change the trajectory of the school. Even if a president makes terrible choices that squander money and bring negative attention to the school, a major research institution will likely suffer at most a small reputational hit. A similar blunder or set of blunders at a small college can easily lead to its closure.

Because the stakes are existential at a small college, there is a natural tendency to avoid taking chances that could lead to disaster. But to succeed, it is almost always necessary to take risks. The conundrum facing the small college president is well illustrated by a historical example from the English Civil War. In November of 1644, the Earl of Manchester said to Oliver Cromwell: "I beseech you let's consider what we do. The King need not care how oft he fights, but it concerns us to be wary, for in fighting we venture all to nothing. If we fight a hundred times and beat him ninety-nine times, he will be King still. But if he beat us but once, or the last time, we shall be hanged, we shall lose our estates, and our posterities be undone" (Wedgwood 1959, 386).

As a result of the poor odds facing small colleges, presidents are often leery of taking large risks. This often plays poorly with trustees or others who desire someone to bring a large vision of great success. And sometimes small colleges are the beneficiaries of existential gambles that pay off successfully. But arguably they are more often the victims of risks that have not been properly calculated. In most situations, a president will be well served to follow the admonition of Edmund Burke (1790 [2009], 9): "Better to be despised for too anxious apprehensions, than ruined by too confident a security." Often, a less expansive vision successfully executed in a sustainable way is a surer way forward than a bold leap into the unknown. This is especially true if the bold leap requires taking on debt or other constraints that reduce future options for the college. To put it succinctly, implementation is part of strategy.

A recurring theme of this book is that economic analysis is fundamentally about constrained optimization: people making themselves as happy as possible subject to limits. Sometimes the decisions that are made are driven by the limits, rather than by the desires. Perhaps the defining characteristic of a successful small college leader is the ability to pick appropriate gambles to accept while saying no to the myriad of attractive gambles presented. The difficulty is compounded because a successful initiative can readily spawn imitators, meaning that any success could be short-lived. We'll return to that issue in chapter 9.

Making Difficult Decisions

The most difficult decisions to make at a small college involve cutting jobs because there is not enough revenue to support the positions anymore. That was the situation I inherited when I became president at Maryville College in 2010. The school had reduced salaries and benefits in the wake of an enrollment decline associated with the Great Recession, but it still had a structural deficit. The budget for the 2010–2011 year was based on enrolling 1,141 full-time students, while the actual enrollment in fall 2010 was 1,060. I arrived in July, a month after the 2010–2011 fiscal year started in June, and immediately organized a process to identify the most important parts of our work and the most effective parts of our work. Implicit in this process was that less important and less effective areas would be reduced or eliminated, but I took the responsibility for doing so.

By October, I had identified the positions and programs to cut. It was difficult for me to make the decision and to stand up in public and announce it but not as difficult as it was for the people who lost their jobs. As a leader, though, I had to consider the need to effectively and sustainably deliver the school's mission.

I haven't told you the other part, though. In addition to cutting positions to balance the budget, I increased compensation for the people who were still employed. The college had reduced its retirement match from 5 percent to 1 percent in 2008, and I restored it to 5 percent beginning in January 2011. This added about $500,000 to the budget cuts needed. In addition, I restored salaries that had been cut in 2008 to their previous level effective in summer 2011, making balancing the next year's budget that much more difficult. How, people asked, could I increase pay for some people while taking jobs away from others? The answer is that not paying people creates the risk of losing them, which can reduce the likelihood of successfully recruiting and retaining the students needed for the school to thrive. As we will see in the next chapter, people who work at small colleges tend to be driven by more than money, but they still have bills to pay. Deferred maintenance in people is even more deadly than deferred maintenance of the physical plant.

Speaking of deferred maintenance of the physical plant, one of the defining features of my presidencies was attention to roof repair and HVAC upgrades. These types of projects do not lead to naming opportunities, ribbon-cutting ceremonies, or national headlines. But omitting the work—as so many schools do—leads to substandard working and living conditions, which in turn hinder the recruitment and retention of faculty, staff, and students.

Being an economist doesn't really give me additional insight into the importance of compensating people fairly, ensuring that revenue is large enough to cover expenses, or what the maintenance priorities are for the physical plant. The emphasis of the profession on the necessity of choice, though, provides a useful perspective on these types of decisions. Every leader must make decisions. Trying to avoid a difficult decision, in many cases, just passes the difficulty on to someone else. Had I chosen not to cut positions or increase salaries, either I or a future president would have been faced with a worsening financial condition or difficulty in retaining key employees.

What Defines a Constrained College?

Williams College had an annual budget of $292 million in 2023–2024 (Chinman and Polanco 2023), compared to an endowment of $3.5 billion at the end of 2022 (National Association of College and University Business Officers 2024). A simple exercise in division tells us that the endowment could cover the annual budget for 12 years even if the school didn't collect any other revenue. Now, to undertake such a task would be more complicated in practice, as there are legal restrictions on the use of endowments. But it illustrates a college that is, for all practical purposes, unconstrained. Williams would likely object to this characterization, because it would like to accomplish goals beyond what is currently offered. In fact, the article cited emphasizes all the cuts needed to keep the budget in balance. If the school was not constrained, it would be a poor steward of the resources provided to it. Burying one's talents, as the parable tells us, is a sure path to condemnation.

A more typical situation is for a college to have an endowment that is a small multiple of the annual operating budget. A standard recommendation is that colleges attempt to grow their endowment to about 5 times the size of the operating budget. At a 5 percent annual spend rate, that would allow the endowment draw to cover about 25 percent of the college's operations. This is largely an aspirational figure, though, for many colleges. Even major research universities can struggle to meet this benchmark. Consider the school where I worked while writing the first draft of this book, Case Western Reserve University. Its endowment as of 2022 was about $2.3 billion, ranking 67th among the schools in the National Association of College and University Business Officers report cited earlier. But its annual budget in 2021–2022 was $1.3 billion, so the endowment is not even twice the size of the budget (Case Western Reserve University 2023). To be clear, I'm not asking for sympathy for an endowment measured in billions of dollars, but it illustrates the challenge of operating according to conservative financial standards.

For enrollment-driven colleges, an obvious place to look for constraints is in the population of potential students. This is not a simple exercise. For on-campus programs, it is possible to estimate the total number of potential students within a radius of the school. And if the focus is further narrowed to traditional students, it is possible to precisely estimate the total number of high school graduates within a radius. But even these figures are imprecise, because there are nuances of academic preparation, family income, and student preferences to consider. (A sophisticated version of this exercise is presented by Nathan Grawe in his 2018 book.) And once we realize that the typical student is not a recent high school graduate and that online programs are also available, estimating the potential enrollment quickly becomes a challenge.

There are many attempts at creating criteria to distinguish struggling and thriving institutions, with a special focus on trying to predict which ones will close. The book by Astin and Lee (1971) is the modern originator of these studies; please see the Suggestions for Further Reading for a few other examples. These analyses are interesting and garner considerable attention but are of limited use to those charged with leading the colleges. The idiosyncrasies of the schools mean that the degree of resilience is almost impossible to identify ex ante, so that two seemingly identical schools can have very different responses to setbacks. Rather than focus on figuring out which schools are especially weak, it is more useful to consider every school as potentially struggling. When even flagship research universities (the University of Arizona and West Virginia University being two prominent examples in recent years) have publicly cut programs and laid off people, the scale of the challenge facing small colleges is clear.

Relaxing Constraints: The Opportunity Cost Exercise

Acknowledging that resources are scarce does not require adopting a nihilistic view toward potential improvement. A helpful exercise in thinking through possible improvements in an environment of scarcity is something I call the opportunity cost exercise. (To be clear, I didn't invent it.) I invite people to identify what they would be able to do if they had an additional $100,000 (or whatever realistic but meaningful number seems appropriate for the setting). After we've reviewed the suggestions and identified a few top ones, I ask the opportunity cost question: Are there activities we can reduce or discontinue to free up the resources needed to implement one or more of these exciting possibilities? Typically, the answer is yes, even though before the exercise few people would have suggested we had any way to reduce or eliminate activities.

A Constraint That Helps?

Small colleges are renowned for their attention and care for every individual. While this is an admirable trait, it can also lead to self-inflicted difficulties. Consider, for example, the case of a student who has not arranged to completely pay for a semester before the semester starts. Often colleges are reluctant to administratively withdraw the student for two reasons. The first reason is the natural sympathy of faculty and staff for a student who perhaps lacks financial resources. The second reason is that college leaders often prefer to keep enrollment as high as possible, even if some of the students enrolled are not actually paying. The result is that a student who is allowed to continue enrolling in courses—and sometimes living on campus and participating in the meal plan—can accumulate a substantial debt.

Students who are financially on the margin in this way are likely candidates to stop out for a period. In some cases, the students will want to transfer to another institution. A barrier to their doing so may be that many colleges withhold transcripts until a student has paid their debt. Especially in cases where the debt has been allowed to grow, it is unlikely that the student will be able to do this. As a result, a college with good intentions (perhaps) has inadvertently hindered the future ability of a student to successfully complete their degree. Colleges who take this route also tend to have a high level of student receivables (money owed but not yet paid) on their books. Usually, when analyzing a business, a high level of receivables is a positive sign. But if those receivables are unlikely to be paid and in fact are the residue of providing services without collecting revenue, they are a sign of poor performance.

There are two main responses to this issue. The first one, which I implemented in both of my presidencies, is to restrict the ability of students to remain enrolled without paying. At both schools, I was told that enrollments would plummet if we required students to pay on time. My response was that operating a college was hard enough without lying to ourselves. If the student can't pay, then they aren't really on track to graduate. We are deluding ourselves about our real enrollment and in the process saddling a student with a potentially unsustainable debt. At both schools, there was almost no impact on enrollment. And because we were small, we were also able to make exceptions in situations where it was warranted. For example, I approved continued enrollment for a student from a country where it was challenging to move funds to the United States. The student argued that the complicated process was being pursued, and their bill would be paid in full—just in a longer time than usual. In that case, the student was right, and it was a positive situation all around. Because we no longer clogged up our information flows with students who were able to pay on time but weren't being given an incentive to do so, we were able to focus on helping the students who truly had special circumstances. Our student receivables also dropped substantially, improving the audited financial position of the college.

The second response that many schools previously followed, withholding transcripts, was framed as a less draconian approach than handing the debt over to a collection agency. In 2024, though, the U.S. Department of Education required that official transcripts be issued for any student covering the payment periods that the student fully paid (see Field 2024). Because it is not easy for colleges to calculate transcripts this way, the practical effect will likely be to eliminate the withholding of transcripts. This is the culmination of a trend in which states have been gradually banning the practice since 2019, when California first acted.

In *The Odyssey*, Odysseus famously tied himself to the mast so he could hear the song of the Sirens without steering his ship into danger. This is an example of a constraint that can provide a benefit. It is possible that the government removing the option of withholding transcripts can similarly lead to positive results. If schools are more thoughtful about allowing students to remain enrolled, then the financial situation for the colleges can improve while at the same students can be assured of more flexibility in pursuing their educational goals.

Returning to an idea introduced in chapter 3, removing transcript holds can be an example of the extensive margin. Students who were previously discouraged from completing their degrees are now more likely to enroll because a financial and administrative hurdle has been reduced. The reduction in traditional-aged students means that colleges who wish to maintain or increase their enrollment—about all of them—need to look in new areas. This regulatory change can help them.

7

Secular Missionaries

Professors at enrollment-driven colleges, particularly small liberal arts colleges founded by religious denominations, were once primarily clergy members. In addition, they performed many of the administrative duties currently filled by professionals. Today, a wide range of higher education professionals fill both faculty and staff roles, and a very small proportion of them are drawn from the ranks of the clergy. However, there are similarities in the motivation of and selection of individuals in these professional roles, which in turn help illuminate certain features of the institutional landscape.

Among the salient characteristics of faculty and staff are low pay, intrinsic motivation related to mission, and faith in humanism as a sort of ersatz religion. These characteristics are directly connected to some important features of higher education. The intrinsic motivation coupled with the lack of financial incentives imply that in many cases the best framework for understanding faculty and staff is as volunteers rather than employees. As we saw in chapter 1, the nonprofit structure of colleges means that faculty and staff can also exert direct influence on the behavior of the college as well as impose costs on administrators who deviate from their preferences.

Some Preliminaries

In 1899, the Board of Maryville College set the salary for its professors at $1,000 per year, a respectable sum at a time when the average salary in the United States was about $700. At that time, every professor at Maryville College was a Presbyterian minister. None of them had earned doctorates in academic subjects, although there were several with doctorates in divinity, either earned or honorific. Adjusting for inflation, the annual salary for those professors was about $31,200 in 2020. In the 2021–2022 academic year, the annual salary for professors at Maryville College was $59,893—still higher than the median salary in the United States of about $54,000 (according to the Bureau of Labor Statistics) but not by as much in relative terms.[1] (Clotfelter's 2017 book presents data showing that faculty salaries at small colleges declined in inflation-adjusted terms between 1970 and 2015.) The financial returns to faculty employment went down in relative terms, and the demographics of the faculty changed considerably. Essentially, the entire faculty was secular and had earned a doctoral or other terminal degree. In addition, a substantial cadre of administrative professionals was now employed to perform duties previously performed by faculty members, including serving as registrar and overseeing student life. The dean of the Maryville College faculty in 1899 also served as registrar, and upon his becoming president in 1901, he kept both of those other positions until replacements were found a few years later.

The trajectory of professorial demographics and compensation at Maryville College is representative of the broad trend in small liberal arts colleges founded by religious denominations. Deborah Rhode (2006, 16) says in a book reviewing the past and present of American professors: "Traditionally, the life of the mind was thought to entail a certain obliviousness to material rewards. In the earliest American colleges, many faculty either had independent sources of income or were individuals with religious backgrounds and modest worldly expectations." There are also parallels with other enrollment-driven institutions, particularly regional public universities. There has been a growing discussion about whether this trajectory is sustainable, especially in light of a prominent body of "quit lit" explaining reasons for leaving academia and a concurrent emphasis on "alt-ac" careers both in graduate training and beyond.

Meanwhile, leaders at enrollment-driven colleges and universities continue to face the challenge of accomplishing their institutional mission with the professional workforce available to them. A better understanding of the nature of that workforce can lead to more effective ways to recruit and motivate talented people. This chapter connects the process that selects people to enrollment-driven institutions to effective leadership. In particular, both the reasons that people join enrollment-driven institutions and the absence of an exit option in the form of lateral mobility imply an emphasis on voice as the primary approach for influencing institutional change. Thus, the emphasis on shared governance and faculty (and staff) participation in institutional decision-making is not an exogenous feature of higher education but rather arises naturally through the matching of individual employees and institutions.

There is a contrast between faculty and staff who can readily move between higher education and other industries. In some academic disciplines (e.g., engineering) and some administrative fields (e.g., accounting), a person can move from college to corporate employment without much change in the nature of the work. Other academic disciplines (e.g., humanities) and administrative fields (e.g., student affairs) require a collegiate employer. I call the former types of positions "market jobs" and the latter "missionary jobs" and use this distinction to explain certain features of college life.

As is true throughout the book, my generalizations are meant to apply to the small colleges that are their focus. Faculty at research institutions are more mobile because they bring funding and prestige that are valuable to the goals of those schools, which fuels a robust market for lateral hires that is not present in small colleges. Additionally, faculty at small colleges with very large endowments deal with different institutional resource dynamics. However, even at research institutions and rich liberal arts colleges, there is a subset of faculty who are not mobile, whether for professional reasons or for family reasons, and the overall analysis here also applies to them.

Why Choose a Missionary Job?

The professors at Maryville College and other small schools are intelligent and highly motivated people who prepared professionally for years, often at elite universities. Why would someone with professional skills that could demand a six-figure salary take a job paying half that amount? There are (at least) three reasons, each of which is tied to perennial themes in discussions about higher education. The first reason is that a person is committed to the teaching mission and finds the nonpecuniary benefits of the work valuable relative to alternative employment that is more lucrative. The second reason is geographic constraints, often tied to joint location decisions by couples. The third reason is a perceived lack of alternatives: people don't believe that they can find worthwhile employment outside of academia. (An extreme characterization of this last reason would be learned helplessness.)

Mission and Quit Lit

People often stereotype economic decisions as focused on maximizing monetary returns. This is inaccurate, as the assumption employed by economists is that people will make decisions that maximize their happiness. (Technically, economists model people as maximizing "utility" because they recognize that some activities might make one unhappy while still contributing to a larger sense of purpose and fulfillment.) While income is often a useful proxy for happiness because it permits people to purchase goods and services they desire, it is not the only reason that people make decisions about employment. Most people want to do good in the world, not just have a job. Thus, a person with the analytical and communication skills to work as a management consultant (for example) might instead choose to work as an English professor because they value the impact on society in the latter profession.

The theme that emerges from this reason is so-called "quit lit," in which educational professionals explain why they are leaving higher education. To my knowledge, there is not an analogous type of literature involving people who have chosen to change careers or industries. If higher education is a calling, one must justify abandoning that call.

Geographical Constraints and the Two-Body Problem

No one is truly free to choose every aspect of their life. For people in committed relationships, one common restriction on choice is being geographically close to one's partner. More broadly, people can be geographically restricted due to family responsibilities, professional opportunities (marine biologists usually find it helpful to be near water, for example), or personal preference (hot summers or cold winters, big city or small town).

There is a long-running discussion in academia about the "two-body problem" in which the challenge of finding suitable employment for a couple is the focus. The rise in assortative matching—people marrying others who are similar in background and education—has led to a substantial increase in partners who both work in higher education. When recruiting professors and professional staff, the question then becomes how to handle the complex negotiations and decision-making both within a relationship and between individuals/households and institutions. An institution that chooses not to try to hire both members of a couple runs the risk of losing excellent faculty and staff. But an institution that hires both members of a couple runs the risk of underperformance because one of the people is not the best fit, as well as the risk of resentment from other people and departments who believe that the position was created at their expense.

One advantage for small colleges in metropolitan areas is that they are often able to benefit from the two-body problem, both from recruiting faculty and staff who are constrained and from the possibility of a partner of a recruited faculty or staff member finding employment nearby. In chapter 3, we identified ways in which colleges that seem to be competing actually complement each other. The proximity of Maryville College to the University of Tennessee, Oak Ridge National Laboratory, and other major employers of well-educated professionals was a tremendous asset when we searched for faculty and staff.

Learned Helplessness and Alt-Ac

Finally, some people who are engaged in the pursuit of academic employment are genuinely unaware of other possibilities. If one has progressed continuously through the educational process, one has most likely been in school from early childhood through their mid-twenties or early thirties, depending on the length of the doctoral program. Beyond this restricted personal experience, one is also surrounded by—and mentored by—people who have spent a lifetime in academia. It is possible not to realize how the skills and experiences honed through rigorous education can translate into nonacademic employment that is fulfilling. Interestingly, there is also evidence that academics are disproportionately the children of academics, with this being true for economics much more than other disciplines. On the one hand, this is unsurprising given the prevalence of following the parent's trade in much of human history, and in fact it is similar to the observation that military service is also highly concentrated. However, it raises questions about the extent to which academics are truly aware of all their options, while also raising the question about whether people who aren't already on the inside have a fair opportunity to become academics.[2]

The theme in the higher education literature that emerges from this reason is the emphasis on "alt-ac" careers and career preparation. The idea is to educate people about how they can translate their experiences into nonacademic settings. The emphasis is both on helping people who have not succeeded in finding the type of academic position they desire (typically a tenure-track faculty position) and on helping graduate students intentionally learn about and prepare for industries other than higher education.

Features of Missionary Jobs

At the risk of overemphasizing a metaphor, I want to explore a few other reasons that college employees are usefully thought of as missionaries. The term immediately conjures images of people enlightening others about the true faith. Some colleges continue to require that their faculty and staff adhere to a faith statement or even a behavioral statement reflecting the school's faith affiliation. Because these schools are steadfastly religious, applying the term "missionary" doesn't seem too jarring.

But even secular institutions can be argued to require adherence to faith statements. A controversial example is the requirement to provide a diversity statement either as part of the application process or as part of the tenure review. Justin McBrayer (2022) summarized his concern about these statements as follows: "Faculty are already overwhelmingly progressive, and given our propensity to evaluate politically charged issues in light of our own biases, it's plausible that requiring job applicants to provide diversity statements further increases the probability that applicants espousing progressive views about the nature of and solutions to diversity-related problems are hired over politically moderate or conservative competitors." Both the legal environment and college practice have been rapidly evolving on this issue. Some prominent elite universities have dropped the requirement for candidates to provide a diversity statement, and multiple states have passed legislation eliminating their use at public universities. The early months of the second Trump administration have accelerated this trend, although the removal of one set of shibboleths might only lead to the institution of others, perhaps under the rubric of "viewpoint diversity."

Another similarity to missionaries has to do with geography. Many small colleges are located in small towns and rural areas. The faculty and professional staff they hire are overwhelmingly educated in metropolitan areas. Beyond the cultural divide associated with educational differences, there is also the cultural divide between urban and rural that continues to loom large in American life. One observer of this divide, David Brooks (2000), chronicles some examples in his book *Bobos in Paradise.* (Interestingly, when I googled "secular missionaries" the first selection is a book by Larry Grubb looking at the Peace Corps and other ways that Americans attempted to influence development in Africa in the 1960s.)

Finally, the curriculum for a missionary is a mix of spiritual and practical. After all, the missionary is sent not only to bring the religious truth but also to improve the lives of the people who are being evangelized. Similarly, educational institutions provide a curriculum that is a mixture of practical (directly linked to career preparation) and spiritual (liberal arts, progressive politics).

Although much of the political heat around college hiring and curricula has focused on public institutions and elite private institutions, the overall picture is similar for less well-known private schools. The faculty and staff employed by Columbia College were not representative of the politics of South Carolina, nor were the secular missionaries at Maryville College representative of East Tennessee. A prominent professor at one of these schools was (in)famously known for publicly stating that she had come to the South to bring civilization. A clearer example of the stereotypical attitude of the missionary is difficult to find.

Missionary Jobs and Compensation

In the simplest model of work, people choose jobs based on the money they will be paid for the work. Of course, the real decisions people make are not that simple, especially because even qualifying for employment in many fields requires years of study or training. Importantly for our purposes, there is considerable evidence that many people are motivated both by the mission of the organization and by the nonpecuniary features of the job. Those features include autonomy in decision-making, a feeling of competence, and a feeling of identity or relatedness to their colleagues (Cassar and Meier, 2018). Workers who are motivated by nonpecuniary factors are especially likely to place a high priority on the perception of being treated fairly, which can include being consulted on important decisions.

The ur-text of some modern critics of academia, William F. Buckley's (1952 [2002]) *God and Man at Yale* highlights the role of nonpecuniary compensation in attracting and rewarding secular missionaries. "The academic community has no illusions about its importance. It may be that this self-recognition is in part responsible for the willingness of so many men and women to suffer the vicissitudes of an incredibly capricious and inequitable pay-scale. There is some reason for the dedication of the educator; primarily, it must stem from his devotion to his work. But in some measure, he is unquestionably fortified by the knowledge that despite the trials and penury of his existence, he is shaping, more directly than the members of any other profession, the destiny of the world." (171–172)

Different people are motivated by different aspects of reward. As a result, people will select which type of employment they desire based on the potential rewards. People who place a premium on job security but not so much on high pay are likely to find the idea of tenure very attractive. By systematically attracting risk-averse individuals, colleges are building in a structural bias for conservatism at the institutional level. This bias can show up in the form of resistance to change in many ways, including the curriculum, disciplinary boundaries, and even such seemingly small issues as what time classes meet.

Economic analysis focuses on the margin, rather than just the average. The typical missionary job has a high degree of meaning and autonomy but a low degree of financial reward. A standard finding is that adding a small amount of reward has a bigger impact if it is in short supply compared to when it is already abundant. An implication of this result is that colleges might be more effective in motivating their missionary workers with monetary incentives rather than an equivalent investment in building meaning or attachment to a mission.

One way for colleges to provide compensation that doesn't require a (substantial) cash outlay is to underwrite professional development for faculty and staff. Economic theory typically predicts that companies will pay for training in activities that are directly related to the company, while employees will pay for more general skills training that they can take with them. If employees are relatively immobile, then from the company's perspective investing in their development can be a way of increasing compensation without recurring salary costs. This is particularly true if the training can be obtained for free or at a low cost—perhaps even from faculty and staff employed at the college.

If a college can't or won't invest money, it risks the possibility of a low-level equilibrium trap. We first saw this concept in chapter 6 when analyzing deferred maintenance in facilities. Here it takes the form of a situation where people are not motivated to work hard, so productivity is low. More commonly, they work hard but not in ways that most effectively advance the mission of the school but rather in ways that are comfortable for them. Yet it would cost a lot to replace them (or it might be impossible at the current wages), so the institution just keeps them. The classic example of this situation is the old joke about the Soviet economy: "We pretend to work, and they pretend to pay us." That cliché might hit uncomfortably close to home on some small college campuses.

Suppose you're now convinced to add some financial incentives for faculty and staff performance. There is still reason for concern. Some behavioral economics and psychology researchers have found that people will make decisions differently based on whether they are thinking in financial terms or in terms of the impact on others.

A widely publicized example is a daycare that started fining parents who were late picking up their children (Gneezy and Rustichini 2000). The result was an increase in late pickups, as parents moved from considering the impact on the daycare workers to weighing the financial costs of the fine. What was even more interesting was what happened when the daycare stopped imposing the fines after a few weeks. Rather than reverting to the original social contract, the late pickup behavior persisted. Establishing a positive culture is difficult—restoring one after it has been disturbed is even harder.

Shared Governance Concerns and Missionary Jobs

No organization is perfect, because every organization is created by and includes people. The best organizations find ways to identify their imperfections and, where possible, to repair them or at least attempt to improve. Albert Hirschman (1970), in his book *Exit, Voice, and Loyalty*, was the first to systematically analyze the possible responses of people to organizational imperfections and in turn the possible responses of the organization. To put it simply, a person can act either by leaving an organization ("exit") or by complaining ("voice"). A person can also do nothing, which is not exactly what his construct of loyalty means. Rather, loyalty activates and empowers voice for those who choose to act.

We already met Hirschman in chapter 3 when investigating the motivation for alumni engagement and giving. The connection between Hirschman's analysis and the importance of shared governance to an academic setting is also immediate. If exit is not possible (for example because of the absence of a market for lateral hires of tenured faculty in teaching colleges), then voice is the only mechanism by which people can attempt to improve their organization. The concern about not being heard is not some sort of academic idiosyncrasy; rather it is a rational response to the structure of the small college work environment. Even in large research universities, there is close attention paid to including faculty voices.

This attention is perhaps most visible when its expectations are not met, as was prominently the case when Purdue University appointed a new president in 2022. The title of an article in one of the main higher education newspapers says it all: "Confirming Faculty Fears, Purdue's Board Chair Says Trustees Chose President Like a Business" (Kelderman 2022). Unlike some other presidential appointments that were criticized by faculty on the basis that the president lacked appropriate credentials, Purdue's president is a paragon of academic and administrative achievement. The objection was solely about the lack of broad campus inclusion in the decision.

As already mentioned, there is something of an "exit" pathway available, as documented in quit lit. Because the typical exit requires leaving academia, it is reasonable to wonder whether it will be effective in its intention to improve conditions for those who remain. It is easier, perhaps, to believe that the person exiting is incapable of succeeding in academia rather than someone who is genuinely concerned. This is one reason that most quit lit pieces include a substantial section identifying how successful the person has been along with their correspondingly bright prospects for the future. Perhaps the most effective quit lit is that written by faculty members who are already tenured, given the semi-mythical status afforded to achieving that condition. A good example is Dolezal (2022).

There is a coincidence in timing that supports my broad hypothesis regarding faculty governance. Deborah Rhode (2006) finds that unilateral presidential and board decision-making declined significantly over the first half of the twentieth century, as "principles of academic freedom and faculty control over curricular and appointment matters became well established" (88). This timing is roughly concurrent with the rise of research universities as well as the increase in secular higher education, so a speculation that shared governance concerns arise naturally from the selection process for secular missionaries is certainly not anachronistic. Ed Glaeser (2002), using the theoretical framework described in chapter 1, also identifies the first half of the twentieth century as marking an important change in the role of administrators. In earlier times, when colleges were driven more by their founders and less by the preferences of the faculty and staff, conflict tended to involve the president siding with the faculty against the board. A modern example is the experience of Steve Pettit at Bob Jones University, as he led the university to meet academic norms including accreditation, prompting backlash from the board and acclaim from the faculty. 3 As time passed and colleges became more what faculty and staff wanted, the conflict tended to involve the faculty and staff against the president and the board.

Another Reason for Voice: Low Cost

If a person is tenured, then there is little likelihood that speaking out will cost them their job. In addition, the advent of social media to complement email as a way to rapidly disseminate whatever a professor wants to say reduces the cost of voice even more. It's much faster to type a message and hit send than to send letters or memos to individuals.

Because most faculty members have considerable autonomy over their time, they also bear a relatively low cost of speaking. The opportunity cost to a president of carefully spending hours in discussion over various issues is the lost chance to raise money for the college, which can lower their chance of getting a raise or perhaps even keeping their job. A professor, particularly one whose income is based on teaching, faces essentially no financial burden, although there is still an opportunity cost in terms of what else they could have done with the time. Because professors are critical thinkers and often like to argue, engaging in detailed discussions can actually be a benefit from their viewpoint rather than a cost.

A friend of mine who was in a leadership position with a law school despaired over the long speeches with which his colleagues consumed hours of time. He proposed, only half in jest, the use of a speaking stick with a limited amount of time. That way, every person would have an equal opportunity to speak and the people who were prone to filibustering or pontificating would at least have a limit. Actually, my friend's proposal was even more sophisticated as it considered the economist's desire to foster mutually beneficial trades. His plan would allow professors who didn't want to talk to give some of their minutes to their more vocal colleagues. To make sure that this opportunity was not abused, his one stipulation was that the donor of the time had to be present to listen to whatever was said.

Why Don't Institutions Improve?

The original motivation for Hirschman's (1970) analysis was to identify ways in which institutions could recover from temporary departures from ideal behavior. Humans—and thus human institutions—are fallible, so mistakes will occur. In some cases, those mistakes are impossible to recover from. But the extreme situation of a college closing (or other institutional dissolution) brings with it a great deal of harm, so finding ways to recover from nonfatal mistakes is a great benefit.

Colleges are full of smart people, some of whom have read Hirschman (and his successors) and surely understand the value of finding ways to recover from missteps. Why, then, do so many dysfunctional situations persist?

The first explanation lies in the unwillingness of people to act (using exit or voice) to remediate errors (Hirschman 1970, 97). Hirschman points out that institutions that impose high costs of exit thereby delay or prevent the use of exit to identify problems. The clearest case of a high exit cost is leaving a tenured faculty position, where one is trading what amounts to lifetime job security for a much less certain outcome. More broadly, the notion that employment outside of academia is less appealing can lead people to stay. The increasing political polarization of the academic workforce is both a contributor to this phenomenon and a symptom of it.

So, if exit isn't likely, why wouldn't voice automatically be activated? After all, that is what I suggested earlier about shared governance. If there are high entry costs, Hirschman points out that the use of voice might be delayed. The notion of cognitive dissonance implies that people are uncomfortable carrying two contradictory ideas around. In this case, the contradictory ideas are that (1) I'm a smart person who has incurred high costs of entry into a desirable field of work, and (2) the work and my workplace are fundamentally flawed. It is more comfortable to blame whatever shortcomings are observed on outside negative actors who don't understand the value of the work and the college.

Another explanation lies in the potential disconnect between actions that an institution will use to improve itself and actions that an individual takes in response to problems. Briefly, if mistakes lead to voice while an institution only responds to exit, then the voice will not be effective. Hirschman (1970, 122) calls this "institutionalized dissent," and while he doesn't mention colleges, the brief description of the problem will likely sound familiar. Who hasn't sat through repeated faculty meetings hearing the same people voicing the same concerns, with no impact on institutional policy? If the people who can successfully address the complaint do not feel any pain from the situation, then just listening to complaints is unlikely to change their minds. Perhaps the combination of exit by tenured faculty members and difficulty in recruiting people can lead colleges to change more readily than any amount of standard committee work. But, as already noted, tenured faculty members are the least likely to exit. And the risk aversion and focus on mission that characterizes the people who join academia are not fertile breeding grounds for decisive leadership that takes responsibility for outcomes.

Implications for Effective College Leadership

In the taxonomy I introduced earlier, senior leadership positions are a market job, regardless of the original professional status of the person. Implicitly, this distinction creates a divide between faculty and administration that is usually not articulated. A dean, provost, or president could make a lateral move, and in fact it is a typical part of the career path. To be most effective, the people in those leadership roles need to consciously take into account both the different job prospects for and the different motivations of the secular missionaries with whom they work.

The recruitment process for a person making a long-term (lifetime) employment commitment is not the same as for someone making a more temporary and contingent commitment. It is vital both to find people who truly resonate with the college's mission and to activate and direct their enthusiasm into productive channels. Even when recruiting for missionary jobs, it is important to remember that there might be alternative motivations for the candidates, so crafting the institutional message requires adapting to individual situations.

An important tension to monitor on campus is between those holding missionary jobs and those holding market jobs. That is not a simple faculty–staff divide, as so often appears in higher education. Especially in cases where the outside options for people have improved rapidly, there can be a difficult decision about whether to increase compensation for the market jobs relative to the missionary jobs, assuming that a general increase in compensation is not feasible. The choice then becomes whether to struggle to recruit people of the quality desired or to create resentment among those whose compensation does not match those of newcomers to the organization. Because those newcomers are also likely to continue to have better outside options while the incumbents are likely to remain, this resentment could develop into a chronic feature rather than a short-term challenge. In my experience, nursing is especially subject to this condition among faculty—and my experience in managing nursing programs predates the COVID pandemic with its resulting increase in nursing salaries. IT is a perennial staffing challenge as well. The alternative, in which key positions are unfilled or performed in ways that do not seem satisfactory, is also difficult, particularly if long-term faculty and staff remember and make invidious comparisons to how things used to be.

In the *Chronicle of Higher Education* article about the Purdue presidential selection (Kelderman 2022), there is criticism of running the university like a business. That criticism is misplaced—there is no choice but to run a university or a small college like a business. The question, though, is what type of business it will be run as. Will it be one that broadly includes its faculty and staff in important decisions or one in which the board and the senior administrators expect everyone to fall in line? My conclusion is that successful colleges will find ways to activate and empower voice, despite the discomfort and potential inefficiencies that result. If the goal is to mobilize the talents and energy of the faculty and staff, then spending extra time to enable them to help craft the institutional strategy and their own part in implementing it can pay dividends far beyond the short-term costs.

Graduate Students as Faculty

A longstanding trend that attracts concern is the increased amount of time required to complete the PhD. More than 50 years ago, Jacques Barzun (1968) reflected on his experience as provost at Columbia University and concluded that the PhD was an excessive requirement for teaching faculty. He recommended instead that only a limited number of professors should complete a doctorate and specialize in research, while professors whose primary responsibility was teaching should stop with a master's degree. One interpretation of extended time-to-degree combined with low compensation for teaching is that Barzun's suggestion has been implemented on an ad hoc basis. What is the difference between hiring a term professor with a master's degree to teach courses at a low salary and hiring a PhD student (with a master's degree) to teach courses at a low salary? Especially if I know that the PhD student is tied to my university for five or more years?

A natural response, then, is for these teachers (or teacher/students) to find ways to amplify their voice. The increase in unionization of graduate students, adjunct faculty, and non-tenure-track faculty can be understood in precisely this way.

Why Do Colleges Still Hire Tenure-Track Faculty?

In the simple stylized model of supply and demand, the price of a product adjusts so that the quantity demanded equals the quantity supplied. In many academic disciplines, there is a substantial excess supply (unemployment) at the existing price, even though the existing price (wage) is low. It seems obvious that a college administration that wanted to use its limited resources most efficiently would hire nothing but adjunct faculty if possible. Beyond the savings in wages, the more tenuous job security would likely reduce the likelihood of faculty voice being mobilized, even given the recent increases in union activity. Why are colleges still hiring tenure-track faculty in missionary job fields?

One answer comes from the work of Nobel Prize-winning economist George Akerlof (1984, 166 ff.). He uses the concept of "gift exchange" from sociology and anthropology to analyze the relationship between employers and employees. The basic idea is that humans are predisposed to reciprocate when someone gives them a gift. If an employer pays a higher wage than the minimum necessary, the employee will work harder than the minimum. It is possible that the additional effort is enough to make it worthwhile for the employer to pay the higher wage.

This theory not only provides one explanation for why colleges continue to offer long-term/lifetime employment in the form of tenure; it also sheds light on the vehement negative response by faculty to the increase in the fraction of adjuncts. The "unpaid labor" such as advising or committee work that is highlighted by faculty both in quit lit and in quiet quitting can be thought of as a gift previously offered to generous employers, now being withdrawn because the employer is no longer perceived as generous.

8

Risk and Uncertainty

The world is uncertain. That makes it difficult to make decisions, especially when those decisions cannot be easily changed. For example, if a college builds a new building anticipating an increase in enrollment, it can't change its mind a year later when enrollment declines. But if the college waits for the actual enrollment to increase before building, it is left overcrowded, which could lead to negative student experiences that cause future enrollment to decline. And of course, even once we learn what this semester's enrollment is, we are still uncertain about future enrollments. How, then, do we make good decisions?

There is a substantial body of economics research on this question. One important contributor to this literature is Ben Bernanke, best known as chair of the Federal Reserve, back when he was a young professor. Bernanke (1983) investigated the question of how companies could make good decisions about irreversible investments in an uncertain world, focusing especially on the question of what kind of information was most useful. Perhaps surprisingly, the answer is that what matters most in making decisions is information about potential downside risk, not information about upside potential. The logic is that companies—colleges—have a choice not only about whether to make an investment but also about when to do so. Deciding not to build a building today preserves the option to build the building (or not) next year. By choosing to wait, the college gives up the benefit of having the building but also avoids the cost of mistakenly building an unneeded building. This option is valuable only if there is a real chance that the investment will be a mistake. In other words, knowing how likely it is that it's a mistake is valuable. This is the so-called "bad news principle," and it is broadly applicable to decision-making under uncertainty.

The bad news principle implies that college leaders, when making irreversible investments, should focus on better understanding the potential bad outcomes. It also means that colleges are more likely to invest if their downside risk is limited. Most small colleges have considerable risks because of their "one semester away from a crisis" financial situation. If their credit and liquidity risk is reduced, they will be more willing to invest.

Investments include not only buildings but also decisions to hire people and even to enroll students. One way of thinking about the pre-tenure faculty evaluation process is that it provides the college with some information about the professor that can mitigate the risk of making a lifetime appointment. Similarly, one impact of government grants and loan guarantees for students is to reduce the risk of a college being left with no revenue if a seemingly risky student enrolls and then doesn't pay. For constrained colleges, identifying and reducing downside risk is crucial to long-term success.

One important point is, for there to be value in waiting, it must be the case that new information will be coming that will help with the decision. Otherwise, waiting is just procrastination or a way of making the decision not to invest by postponing the decision indefinitely.

Risk vs. Uncertainty

Frank Knight is a name unknown to most people but familiar to economists because of his association with the distinction between risk and uncertainty proposed in his 1921 book, *Risk, Uncertainty, and Profit*. Risk, according to Knight, represents measurable unknowns. For example, if one is flipping a fair coin, there is risk, as the result could be heads or tails with a 50 percent probability.

Uncertainty, though, is unmeasurable. Many—perhaps most—of the decisions that we make daily involve situations where probabilities of specific outcomes can't be quantified. To extend the example of flipping a coin, suppose that the coin had an unknown number of sides, some of which were heads and some tails. Given that information, how would you assess the probability of a head or tail coming up? While this example might be awkward, it captures the heart of the concept of Knightian uncertainty. In broader culture, the idea of uncertainty has surfaced under the term "black swan" popularized in the book of the same name by Nassim Taleb (2007). Because humans are uncomfortable with uncertainty, he argues that we are surprised when it manifests itself and we construct explanations with the benefit of hindsight that transform the uncertainty into risk.

The difference between uncertainty and risk is not strictly academic, as it has implications for how people behave—and how they should behave. Risk can be understood and sometimes reduced. The insurance industry is based on this idea. Because the risks of property damage can be quantified by insurance underwriters, mutually beneficial trade is possible between those who want to reduce risk (people and companies, including colleges) and those willing to take it on (insurance companies).

Although risk can be addressed, it is important to realize that people are generally not good at dealing with risk. An important line of research in economics that overlaps with psychology is behavioral economics, which uses experiments to understand the ways in which people make decisions. When faced with situations of risk, there are predictable ways that people will deviate from the best responses. For example, the phenomenon of "anchoring" finds people leaning too heavily on the current situation as a prediction of the future or a gauge of what to expect as normal. The phenomenon of "framing" finds people making different decisions depending solely on how a question is posed. And perhaps most worrisome, people tend to believe that risk is less than its true amount. When asked to indicate a range in which they expect outcomes to occur, people are usually much too confident that the outcome will occur in a narrow range, ignoring the possibility of chance or even their own ignorance. This phenomenon is not new. In the early Han dynasty (207 B.C.E.–220 C.E.), eight Taoist sages were invited by the king of Huainan to discuss what they had learned. Their teachings were recorded and compiled, and I quote one appropriate excerpt: "When the unexpected happens, the ignorant are surprised; knowers don't think it strange" (Cleary 1990, 60). To summarize, people look at risk in biased ways that often do not even recognize their true exposure to risk.

Uncertainty is different than risk. Before becoming famous for helping leak the Pentagon Papers, Daniel Ellsberg was a social scientist who developed an experiment that linked psychology and economics and highlighted the difference between risk and uncertainty. In the experiment people were given a choice of a risky situation and an uncertain situation that had less risk. Systematically, people chose the risky situation. As a classroom instructor, I regularly replicated this experiment with my students. His discovery is known as the Ellsberg paradox, and it shows that people would rather face situations of risk than uncertainty, even at the hazard of magnifying some of the risk. Known unknowns are preferred to unknown unknowns, and as Taleb emphasizes in *The Black Swan*, people often want to retrospectively reduce the unknowns to knowns. In addition to this important finding, the Ellsberg paradox illustrates the importance of close collaboration between disciplines and communication across disciplines—a hallmark of the liberal arts approach championed at most small colleges.

While experimental evidence from the relatively controlled setting of the laboratory is interesting, it is not sufficient to convince most people. Fortunately—although that's not really the right word—we have a prominent example of uncertainty regularly dominating the news. Anthropogenic climate change is a large-scale, long-term set of issues that has, ironically, often generated more heat than light in public discussion.

The standard approach that economists use to analyze long-term situations involving the future is cost–benefit analysis. The usual framework of such analysis is that it assumes that we know what the probability is for various outcomes—in other words that we are in a situation of risk. However, there are some fundamental uncertainties involved in the potential impact of climate change. In particular, the possibility of strong threshold effects where a small change in temperature leads to a dramatic shift in some other condition means that the standard cost–benefit analysis might not apply. As a result, much attention is focused on the possibility of extreme events and understanding how uncertainty, rather than just risk, can best be mitigated. In an article discussing an important analysis of the potential impact of anthropogenic climate change, Harvard professor Martin Weitzman (2007, 703) summarizes, "The basic issue here is that spending money to slow global warming [is] about how much insurance to buy to offset the small chance of a ruinous catastrophe that is difficult to compensate by ordinary savings." This conclusion does not automatically imply any specific government policy will be better than actions by private individuals—after all, governments are elected by and composed of people. Rather, it implies that we should look for approaches that recognize with appropriate humility our limited ability to foresee all possible outcomes. As Weitzman says, "Gathering information about [thicktailed] uncertainties representing rare climate disasters (and developing a realistic emergency plan were they to materialize) should be a priority of research" (704).

While climate change caused by people is an important question, it is not the only complication caused by the fact that we deal with individuals rather than automata. Another influential economic thinker, Joseph Schumpeter, said, "Without committing ourselves either to hero worship or to its hardly less absurd opposite, we have got to realize that, since the emergence of exceptional individuals does not lend itself to scientific generalization, there is here an element that, together with the element of random occurrences with which it may be amalgamated, seriously limits our ability to forecast the future" (McCraw 2007, 475–476).

As is so often the case, we can find antecedents of modern analysis in the Bible. The book of James (4:13–14) reminds us that the future is always uncertain. "Go to now, ye that say, Today or tomorrow we will go into such a city, and continue there a year, and buy and sell, and get gain: Whereas ye know not what shall be on the morrow. For what is your life? It is even a vapour, that appeareth for a little time, and then vanisheth away."

In *Risk, Uncertainty, and Profit,* Frank Knight (1921, 313) says, "We live in a world full of contradiction and paradox, a fact of which perhaps the most fundamental illustration is this: that the existence of a problem of knowledge depends on the future being different from the past, while the possibility of the solution depends on the future being like the past."

Despite this uncertainty, it is vital to move forward with faith, as the nature of uncertainty is that it is never completely resolved. In *Julius Caesar,* William Shakespeare gives Brutus something memorable to say on this subject (Act IV, Scene 3, 218–224): "There is a tide in the affairs of men. Which, taken at the flood, leads on to fortune; Omitted, all the voyage of their life is bound in shallows and in miseries. On such a full sea are we now afloat, and we must take the current when it serves, or lose our ventures."

Creativity is inextricably linked to faith. As the author of Hebrews says (11:1), "Faith is the substance of things hoped for, the evidence of things not seen." When we create, we bring something to the world that was not seen before, something that we and perhaps others had hoped for.

This creativity is also inextricably linked to knowledge. In one of my favorite books, *His Master's Voice*, the Polish author Stanislaw Lem (1968 [1983]) poses the question, what would happen if we received a message from another world and couldn't decipher it? The narrator introduces the story by including a criticism of how people often approach science, "acting like a child who thinks the names of the stars and planets are written on them, and that the astronomers read these off though their telescopes" to introduce the theme that true research and discovery involve creativity (20–21). Faith and learning are complements, and small colleges that continue to relate to their faith tradition will flourish in their distinctive blending where both aspects of human development are taken seriously.

A liberal arts education prepares students for risk, by helping them gain knowledge and develop the habits of study that will lead to a lifelong ability to grow in knowledge, and for uncertainty, by helping them gain wisdom (including the wisdom to distinguish risk and uncertainty) and grow in faith. Let us study to develop knowledge and wisdom so that we can go forth prepared for a world of risk and uncertainty.

Faculty Hiring and Tenure

In my roles as chief academic officer and as president, I met with every finalist for a faculty position. There is almost nothing more important for a college than hiring the next cohort of faculty members. A professor's career can last many years, influencing both colleagues and students not only during their time on campus but also for decades after they retire. Thus, each person hired represents a chance to have an impact on the college and community for perhaps a century. In many ways, the fundamental strategic responsibility of college leaders is to attract, develop, and retain top talent.

It is difficult to identify the right people, in part because we are having to make decisions based on incomplete information (risk and uncertainty) and in part because of incomplete contracts (discussed in chapter 2). It is helpful to examine faculty hiring through the lens of economic theories about decision-making when there is incomplete information and incomplete contracts.

A distinctive feature of faculty employment at most colleges is tenure. While this is not the completely unaccountable lifetime employment of myth, it is nevertheless a situation that requires special effort by the college to terminate. In economic terms, tenure is a form of job insurance. And insurance raises questions of adverse selection (are we insuring the right people?) and moral hazard (insurance changes incentives).

Adverse Selection

Typically, people know different things. For example, a person knows how healthy they are, while an insurer knows how likely they are to fulfill their promises to the person they insure. The technical term for such a situation is "asymmetric information." The presence of asymmetric information can make it difficult for people to reach agreements. One reason is the problem of adverse selection. In the health insurance example, the challenge is that the less healthy people will want insurance while the healthiest don't, which might make it impossible for the insurance company to stay in business. (George Akerlof won a Nobel Prize for carefully articulating this challenge.) What about the case of tenured faculty?

The college hopes that everyone who applies to work there does so because they value the mission and will contribute to accomplishing it. Unfortunately, it might be the case that people apply for other reasons the college can't observe. Consider a simple situation where there are two jobs—consultant and professor—and people are qualified for both jobs. The consultant job pays much more than the professor job, but it's riskier. In this situation, the people who apply for the professor job will systematically be more risk-averse than the people who apply for the consultant job.

This example, while extremely simplified, is nevertheless instructive. The potential security of a tenured position will attract risk-averse individuals. Some of the implications of this self-selection have already been explored in chapter 7.

One way insurance companies try to influence who they deal with is through review processes. If colleges wanted to hire faculty who are less risk-averse, they could do so in several ways. One way might be to offer contracts that don't include tenure. Another way might be to look at a professor's background for evidence that they are willing to take risks. A deeper challenge is that, if colleges have systematically recruited risk-averse faculty for years/generations, where will it find people interested in leading an effort to change the risk preferences of the faculty?

Moral Hazard

Incentives matter. In the context of insurance, that truism turns up in the idea of moral hazard. This is a technical term, not an ethical judgment, referring to the idea that insurance changes the incentives facing the person who is insured. Consider, for example, the impact of no car insurance on driving behavior. It might well be the case that a person would be more careful if they knew they would bear the full cost of any accident.

The moral hazard of tenure is that professors can pursue their own desires rather than promote the mission of the college. To an extent, this is just another example of the principal–agent problem we saw in chapter 2. Framing it as moral hazard, though, illuminates the pre-tenure process as one of trying to identify people who are intrinsically motivated to behave in ways that advance the college's mission. An arduous multiyear process is likely to be appealing only to someone who values the work, especially given the relatively small financial rewards (although there is value in job security even at a low salary).

Even if the process successfully selects for people who value the educational mission, there is still the possibility for professors to adjust their work to their own benefit at the margin. (As an anonymous reviewer pointed out, it is probably not true that every professor gives 100 percent effort to every class.) The only way this sort of adjustment would not be possible is if the school had inflexible rules regarding behavior. But if it were possible to set strict and uniform rules about activities, then hiring independent-minded professionals doesn't seem to make much sense.

One way insurance companies respond to the presence of moral hazard is to require the insured party to face some cost if the insured event occurs (copay or deductible). Another way is to have some sort of monitoring, such as a smartphone app that keeps track of how fast one drives. While it isn't obvious (to me, at least) how to implement a financial copay or deductible for faculty behavior, it is certainly possible to implement forms of monitoring. The widespread use of post-tenure review and the attention paid to various forms of high-stakes testing (such as professional license exams for graduates) can be understood as institutional responses to moral hazard. Awards for outstanding performance in teaching, research, or service can also be understood as a sort of "anti-deductible" where faculty are rewarded for exemplary service in advancing the mission as opposed to being penalized for shirking.

Admissions

A common complaint is that all colleges sound alike in their advertising. Is there a school that doesn't claim to have small classes taught by caring faculty that put students first? In fact, for a board meeting when I was president, we illustrated this point by presenting some alleged proposed catchphrases for our school. After some positive comments from board members about how we had captured the essence of our distinctiveness, we showed the other schools that were already using those phrases, which included both small colleges and large research universities. The point is that a lot of college advertising seems quite uninformative.

Given that choosing to attend a college is a substantial investment of money and time, the question is why students don't demand better. After all, applying the bad news principle to their decision suggests that they find information that reduces their downside risk to be very valuable. A school that could credibly communicate that it is not risky would stand to benefit relative to other schools. To be sure, "credibly" is doing a lot of work in the previous sentence. One challenge is that different people have different preferences about their educational experience. What is perfect for one person would be a disaster for someone else.

Even worse for informative advertising, college is an experience good. In other words, it is almost impossible to know in advance what the experience will be like. Even the most assiduous prospective student will be surprised by the actual experience of the school. Thus, it is challenging to determine the true opportunity cost of attending one college instead of taking alternative options.

So it's difficult. But that is not a complete explanation of why college advertisements are uninformative. Nobel Prize winner George Akerlof presents one general class of explanation based on cognitive dissonance. Essentially, once a student decides to attend a school (or a faculty member joins it), they have a psychological incentive to believe it is a better place than objective information suggests. This is especially true in the case of goods or services when it can be hard to determine whether someone's needs are met. "People like to feel that they are attractive, socially adept, and intelligent. It makes them feel good to hold such beliefs about themselves. Ads facilitate the process—if the person buys the advertised product" (Akerlof 1984, 140–141). Yes, all admissions materials—and alumni magazines—look alike. And that is because their primary role is not to communicate to prospective students regarding the distinctive features of the school but to communicate to current and former students that they made a superior choice.

COVID-19: Uncertainty

It is hard to imagine a clearer example of uncertainty than the pandemic that transformed American society beginning in 2020. I remember vividly the disruption caused, and especially the frustration at not knowing the right thing to do. To illustrate how quickly everything changed, consider my itinerary during the second week of March 2020. On Wednesday, March 11, I interviewed for a job and then traveled home by plane. At the interview, none of us shook hands, but no one was wearing masks. On Friday, March 13, I chaired a conference call of the presidents in our athletic conference, during which we cancelled the rest of the spring athletics season. Shortly afterwards, Maryville College extended spring break by a week to transition classes from in-person to online.

College leaders must weigh probabilities daily in order to evaluate their options. For this to be possible, there must be clear options, reasonable estimates of the costs and benefits of adopting those options, and plausible beliefs about the relative likelihood of different events. That is just part of operating in an atmosphere of risk. The events surrounding the onset of the pandemic did not provide a scenario of risk. At that point in time, we were making decisions without knowing things as basic as what the transmission mechanism for the virus was. For example, a great deal of attention was paid to cleaning surfaces, while we now know that transmission was almost entirely airborne. We also were making decisions in a condition of financial uncertainty. I have already explained how the revenues generated from residential students are crucial to successfully operating a college. We didn't know whether there would be the type of government support that eventually arrived, and we didn't know whether and when we would be able to open residence halls again.

What did we do? First, we were as transparent as possible. Admitting ignorance is unpleasant, but doing so as part of an overall plan to identify the best possible options is vital. Attempting to claim knowledge in an atmosphere of uncertainty is a way to undermine credibility. Second, we worked to maintain flexibility. Because new information and possibilities were continually coming to light, we had to be ready to stop doing something and start doing something else. Colleges are essentially conservative places, wedded to traditional practices and schedules, so this was stressful. Third, we tried to imagine a wide range of possible scenarios. In a risky environment, we can usually identify a likely trend and then construct reasonable alternatives from it. In an uncertain environment, it is crucial to think well beyond the typical possibilities.

In my opinion, what COVID-19 did was clarify that we are always in an uncertain environment rather than a risky environment or, more precisely, that there is global uncertainty and local risk. After all, before the pandemic there was the Great Recession, and before that 9/11 and its aftermath. When listening to alumni, faculty, and staff, there is often some sort of implicit or explicit allusion to a utopian time where everything worked well and an attitude that we just need to return to that time. Having immersed myself in the histories of two small colleges, I was unable to discover such a time ever actually existed. Adopting a stance that we are in a world of uncertainty does not mean that we should abandon careful analysis of risky options. Rather, it means that we should be humble not only about our choices but also about the information and analysis upon which we base our choices: "There are more things on Heaven and Earth, Horatio, than are dreamt of in your philosophy" (Shakepeare's *Hamlet*, Act I, Scene 5).

Flexibility vs. Rigidity

The unpredictable and ever-changing nature of the world would seem to call for corresponding agility and flexibility in response. While this conclusion has much to justify it, there is in fact an argument for reducing flexibility as a response to uncertainty.

Perhaps the most famous example of reducing flexibility to pursue goals is Odysseus lashing himself to the mast so that he can listen to the Sirens without wrecking his ship. Small colleges don't operate in a mythological environment, but there are nevertheless lessons to be learned from Odysseus.

Economists frame this issue as the time inconsistency of optimal plans. That's a mouthful, but the basic idea is straightforward. Suppose that I am working to complete a book and decide that I will spend the next morning drafting a section about the value of flexibility. But the next morning is beautiful, so I decide instead to spend the morning outside taking a walk. This is a nice way to spend a morning but not the best way to achieve my goal of finishing a book. Some form of commitment device would help me overcome this short-term temptation as I work on my long-term goals. The phrase "time inconsistency" refers to the fact that I'm making different decisions at different times. In this example, I decided on the previous evening to write the book the next morning but the next morning I decide to go for a walk instead.

Colleges face these challenges regularly. As the world changes, it is tempting to alter the curriculum and other features rapidly to respond to trends, even if that is not consistent with the long-term trajectory desired by some parts of the college community. As we saw in chapter 3, alumni are affected by the perception of the school for decades after they graduate. Therefore, they have reasons to want assurance that the quality will remain high (as they define quality) before making financial contributions or volunteering on behalf of the school. Various forms of institutional rigidity can help assure them that the college will not move away from the ideal. Most endowment gifts are restricted, providing the donor with assurance that they will go to the desired use even after the donor is gone. By providing this commitment, the college is able to attract financial gifts that enhance its future flexibility and resilience.

To harken back to chapter 7, one of the most visible forms of institutional rigidity is tenure for faculty members. The loss in flexibility that results from tenure, in this analysis, could be more than balanced by the gain in terms of institutional commitment to a particular approach in pedagogy and curriculum.

Colleges with covenant relationships with religious denominations provide another example of institutional rigidity. Again, the tradeoff is between navigating evolving curricular and co-curricular trends and maintaining good standing with the religious sponsor or partner. Because, in some cases, members of the religion are important sources of students (hence tuition) or financial contributions, colleges can have a financial incentive to clearly lash themselves to the mast, thus avoiding the temptation of secular fashion.

9

Herding

A defining feature of higher education in the United States is the heterogeneity of institutions. While the differences among schools make it more difficult for students to find the best fit because they have so many options, those same differences make it possible for students to find a great fit because they have so many options. It is interesting, therefore, to consider situations in which institutions seem to do their best not to distinguish themselves. In the previous chapter, we saw ways in which admissions materials can be very similar. But the phenomenon extends beyond admissions.

There used to be a cliché about investment managers: "No one gets fired for buying IBM." In other words, sometimes it is safest to follow conventional wisdom, even if it is not your personal preference. The application of this cliché to college leadership is immediate. Publicly making choices that are different from what other schools are doing is difficult. Not only is it difficult to be different because you lose the advantage of learning from what others are doing, but it is also difficult because any failure will be clearly attributable to you. Even though you might not jump off a cliff just because your friends do, you still might be tempted to lead your college off a cliff because your peers are too.

Rankings

I'm so old, I had to choose a college before the U.S. News and World Report rankings existed. Somehow, though, everyone was still able to figure out certain things about schools. I remember in elementary school in the early 1970s that there were book covers that depicted the academic seals of Ivy League institutions, presumably to foster high-status academic aspirations. It's not as if invidious comparisons among schools started with the inaugural U.S. News ranking in 1983. In fact, many of the criteria used in the U.S. News rankings have long been publicly available, including the size of endowment, test scores of incoming students, graduation rates, faculty/student ratios, and so on.

There are more essays criticizing the rankings than can be easily summarized here. Notably, though, very few institutions have really done much about them. Reed College has long been an outlier in its refusal to participate in the "beauty contest" (peer rating of other schools) part of the U.S. News process as well as its refusal to provide information. Beginning in 2023, a series of high-profile schools have abandoned participation in the law school rankings, medical school rankings, and undergraduate college rankings. While these developments—and the arguments about rankings—are interesting, they aren't really the key issues that an economic analysis would identify. So rather than delve into the nitty-gritty of the U.S. News ranking system, I focus on some broader concerns.

People and institutions respond to incentives. Once the rankings existed and institutions could see that they seemed to affect enrollment, there was an incentive to strive for a higher ranking. Ideally, that would mean performing the institutional mission more effectively and being rewarded by the ranking process. In practice, it meant reverse engineering the ranking process to artificially enhance the items being measured.

The easiest way to artificially improve one's ranking is strategic voting. Because the peer rating is a substantial fraction of the rank, a person interested in increasing their school's rank should rate it highly and rate all the other schools low. I don't personally know anyone who admits doing so, but because the ratings are not publicly revealed, I suspect some people have voted strategically.

A more complicated approach is to revise institutional practices in ways that don't cost much but have a substantial impact on rankings. One example is to focus on increasing the fraction of courses with low enrollments, typically defined as those under a certain threshold. If the threshold is twenty-five, then making sure that classes that once had twenty-six (or thirty) students are now under twenty-five can improve the ratings without much cost. Another notorious example is the percentage of alumni who give to the school. I know personally of at least one college that would push for tiny contributions (such as $1) to increase that percentage. This is not a cost-effective way to increase philanthropic support for a school, but it might be a cost-effective way to improve in the rankings. Two entertaining accounts of how the reverse engineering of rankings works in practice are Kutner (2014) and Burd (2024).

The people in charge of the U.S. News rankings are smart enough to recognize these incentives. They are also smart enough to know that if they leave the rankings determinants the same every year, then the ranks will likely not change (much), which will reduce the incentive for people to buy the new edition of the magazine. As a result, there is an annual game of colleges and other commentators decrying the rankings formula followed by U.S. News adjusting their formula. For example, the 2024 version increased the weight of a school's success in graduating students from different backgrounds and removed the alumni giving category (along with a couple of other categories). This sounds dramatic, but it only affected about 16 percent of the ranking formula, and the measure of "different backgrounds" is not clearly explained.[1]

Can't we revise the rankings to reflect what people really care about? Because of the commercial success of *U.S. News & World Report,* multiple other publications have entered with their own version. Examples include *Washington Monthly*, focusing on service; other rankings emphasizing different dimensions of quality such as veteran friendliness; *Princeton Review* identifying party schools, etc. These have the same basic problems as *U.S. News & World Report* but serve a purpose for schools by making it possible for them to highlight positive results because people can't look at everything. The most cynical version of the rankings system is the variety of "pay to play" certifications, such as College of Distinction. While the certifications are nominally based on recommendations and evaluation criteria, a school pays for the right to use the branding.

More broadly, any effort to eliminate rankings is doomed by the natural human propensity to make invidious comparisons. In every sphere of human activity, there is a tendency to ascribe high status or low status to various people, activities, products, or institutions. And once high status is identified, it is natural for others to emulate the high-status institution. An influential early analysis of this question was provided by Thorstein Veblen (1899 [1953]). This process naturally extends to higher education. One criticism of rankings is that they flatten the discourse about higher education, as every other institution tries to imitate higher-ranked schools rather than working to be a better version of themselves. But if *U.S. News and World Report* stopped issuing rankings tomorrow, this issue would not disappear. Instead, there would just be some other way of ascribing status that would be used to rank schools with the same negative (and perhaps occasionally positive) impact on institutional incentives to improve. A recent example is the emergence of Hillsdale College among Republican politicians as an alternative Platonic ideal to Harvard.

Zero-Sum vs. Positive-Sum Thinking

Perhaps the worst feature of rankings is that they are a zero-sum activity. Rankings are an example of a positional good, in which the only way for one person or institution to do better is for someone else to do worse. That is the definition of a zero-sum activity.

Many enjoyable pastimes are zero-sum, including board games like chess and athletic competitions like baseball. There is a winner and a loser. However, much of the world is not zero-sum. If the Cleveland Orchestra practices really hard and improves its performances, that does not take away from the quality of the Chicago Symphony. All that happens is that more people can enjoy higher quality music—a positive-sum situation. The question, then, is whether higher education is more like chess or music.

Not only is higher education more of a positive-sum situation, but the diversity of colleges means that in many cases it is like trying to compare the quality of a chess player to the quality of an orchestra. Yes, one can develop a measurement to rank them, but it is unlikely to help people decide how to spend their leisure time. In the wake of the success of the U.S News rankings, a large and still growing number of alternative rankings have been promulgated. (Ironically, this is an example of emulating a high-status institution by creating a supposedly distinctive product.) They are fundamentally flawed because they are applying zero-sum logic to a positive-sum situation. To see this point, let us suppose for a moment that the U.S. News rankings are a perfect measure of the relative quality of colleges. Now suppose that every college works very thoughtfully and diligently to improve itself, and they all improve by the same amount. There is no change in the rankings, even though there is considerable change (improvement) to the experience of students.

Because of the heterogeneity of schools and people and the somewhat arbitrary nature of some of the measures, an alternative suggested approach is grouping schools rather than ranking them. One of the prominent ranking organizations, *Money Magazine*, took that approach beginning in 2023.[2]

One way to make sure you are ranked highly is to carefully choose your comparison group. I am taller than everyone who is shorter than 5'10", for example. Is this so different from a school touting its rank among some carefully selected subset of schools?

It is impossible for every school to be above average, but it is almost impossible to find a school's website lacking a claim to being above average.

Interestingly, some schools compare themselves to higher-ranked institutions. Perhaps this reflects an aspirational approach, or perhaps it represents an attempt to gain status by claiming to be comparable to the other school. June (2022) and Elias (2024) provide evidence on the patterns of comparison.

It is not easy to identify the appropriate comparison schools, even if one were so inclined. A tool that economists use to define the extent of a market is cross-price elasticity. Cross-price elasticity is the impact on the demand for College A if College B changes its price. If the two are truly competitors, then the demand should increase for College A if College B increases its price, all else being held equal. But how do we observe this outcome in practice? The best research evaluates student decisions among schools. Here's the idea: if a student is admitted to two schools and faces the same net cost, then the school they choose is better. If a lot of students are analyzed using careful statistical techniques, these comparisons can be extrapolated into a ranking. Such an exercise was carried out for 3,240 high school students by a group of economists (Avery et al. 2013). Unsurprisingly, Harvard ended up in first place. But there were some interesting findings elsewhere in the ranks, including a broader range of large and small, public and private colleges and universities than usually found at the top of U.S. News rankings.

Standing Out from the Herd

As an economist, I am most attracted to arguments based on advancing the self-interest of individuals, even when the goal is to make society better. Having already hinted at the difficulties of being distinctive, what are the practical and selfish advantages?

One important advantage of being distinctive is that it makes it possible to collect more revenue from students or attract more students. A recurring theme is the need to generate revenue to pay for programs. A college that is perceived to be distinctive will have a lower elasticity of demand for its product. In other words, it will lose fewer students if it raises its price compared to a college that is not perceived as distinctive. It can also attract students who feel strongly about the distinctive elements.

A related advantage—almost a corollary but worthy of its own paragraph—is the need for small colleges to compete on some dimension other than cost. Many small colleges tout their affordability, and the extent of tuition discounting indicates their willingness to invest heavily in this area. However, competing on cost alone runs the risk of being undercut on price. The most dramatic example of that undercutting has been the rise of "free" college programs in various states, typically through last-dollar scholarship programs for community college students. It is difficult to compete with free. Interestingly, when one looks at the fine print of these programs, one finds that they aren't really changing the financial calculation for many of the people (especially Pell Grant recipients) who are nominally being targeted. So small colleges have already been competing with free and should continue to emphasize the net benefits and distinctive elements of their programs.

A fundamental appeal of small colleges is their size and the opportunities for students that result. While each student chooses a college for idiosyncratic reasons, the commonality among those who choose small colleges is typically the ability to pursue multiple activities at a high level. This is clearest in intercollegiate athletics. At Maryville College, we enrolled about 400 varsity athletes in a student body of about 1,200. The University of Tennessee, with over 20,000 undergraduates, had about 700 varsity athletes. Athletes were about 10 times as large a percentage of the student body at Maryville as they were at the University of Tennessee. Granted, the Maryville students were much less likely to pursue professional careers as athletes. But they were able to pursue a college education while continuing to engage in a sport that they loved. There are similar situations in music, art, theater, and community service. For several years during my time at Maryville, one of the top performers in the theater program was a biochemistry major. And typically, about half of the (rigorous, auditioned) concert choir consisted of students who were not music majors. (Full disclosure: while I attended a research university, it was a small one, and I was able not only to pursue my academic interests but also play intercollegiate soccer and play piano for musical theater productions.)

Economists are not invited to parties because they always point out that there are costs as well as benefits that result from every decision. I already mentioned the challenge that leading away from the herd increases accountability. A more subtle issue is that one must be empowered to lead a college away from the herd. It is not enough for a president to believe in something; it is not even enough for them to speak about it. They need to be hired and retained by a board of trustees, and they need to engage a critical mass of faculty and staff on campus, or any initiative will not progress. As we saw in the general model of college governance introduced in chapter 1, the president does not get to make decisions in isolation. Vision without a budget is a dream. A distinctive view without bringing along sufficient allies is a voice crying in the wilderness.

Avoiding Stampedes

Another problem with being distinctive arises when there is success. In this case, the herd stampedes toward you. Any success can be short-lived unless you are able to make your distinction difficult to emulate. Even if you create a distinctive program, it won't stop other schools claiming to be doing something comparable. Obstacles to other colleges copying your innovation are called entry barriers. The name suggests the requirement to erect such barriers, but the barriers might be intrinsic to the program.

The engineering program at York College of Pennsylvania is a good example of a program with substantial entry barriers. The program (patterned after that at Rochester Institute of Technology) includes a required set of industry placements—three semesters in a program that covers four calendar years. There is not only the institutional challenge of administering such a program, but, more importantly, there is the challenge of finding a strong group of industry partners willing to employ students. This is a major commitment on the part of the employers, although it comes with the benefit of potentially reducing their costs of recruiting and training engineers.

The largest graduate program at Columbia College (in South Carolina) is a good example of the challenge of creating entry barriers. The master's degree in trauma-informed education is a careful integration of social work and education, bringing best practices in building resilience together with pedagogical development. The program was developed over several years by the social work and education faculty, and it was launched in May 2020. Because of the impact of the pandemic, it landed on receptive soil, and the program had a waiting list for its first couple of years even without much marketing. However, because of the pandemic, many graduate programs started touting their programs as "trauma-informed" to attract students. Because there is not a standard definition of what it means for a program to be trauma-informed, the only entry barrier is to add the phrase to a program's marketing outreach.

One of the key insights that economists bring is the notion of general equilibrium. This is a phrase that just means that it is not sufficient to look at the immediate direct impact of an action. Rather, we must account for indirect impacts as people react to the action. If your innovation is easy to emulate, the equilibrium outcome is that it will not remain distinctive.

Data-Driven Decisions

A mantra among small colleges is that it is vital to make data-driven decisions. In other words, people should focus on the actual results as opposed to just anecdotes or adhering to past practices. This is undoubtedly good advice. But, like most good advice, it is easier to give than to follow. The combination of risk-averse individuals being selected into academia (as discussed in chapter 7) and the perceived safety of following past practices and not deviating from other schools lead to considerable challenges for the leader who wants to make data-driven decisions that differ.

As the saying goes: it's not what you don't know that's the problem; it's what you know that isn't so. There is a growing economics literature comparing the predictions of experts on the impact of certain decisions with the actual impact of those decisions. One of the more dramatic examples that is especially salient in a small college context is a paper carefully measuring the effect of a standard approach to increasing donor retention (Samek and Longfield 2023). A common "best practice" in fundraising is to make thank-you calls to donors as a supplement to the standard tax receipt and thank-you notes. The idea is that this personal touch will deepen their engagement, leading to continued gift giving. In a study that incorporated the experiences of 500,000 new donors, Samek and Longfield found that the calls had no impact on retention of donors, which was about 30 percent both for the control group who didn't receive calls and the treatment group who received calls. This was a stark contrast to the 80 percent increase in retention predicted by fundraising professionals. While the reason for the large discrepancy between prediction and outcome is not known for sure, the implication of the study is clear. If the calls have any cost at all—and the estimate was about $1 per phone call—then the net benefit of making the calls is less than zero. While one study is not sufficient to prove the ineffectiveness of a widely used approach, it at least suggests that there could be benefits in breaking away from the herd.

Let me give another example that illustrates the challenge in adopting nonstandard approaches. More than ten years ago, I read an article by a former colleague about using the ACT to predict college success (Bettinger et al. 2013). At the time, I was president of a high sticker price/high financial aid college in a state where the

ACT was the most widely used standardized test. Eric Bettinger and his coauthors found that they could better predict student success by using two of the subscores (reading and math) of the ACT rather than using the composite score. Given that we were awarding millions of dollars in institutional aid based on ACT scores, it seemed like an opportunity to refine our approach and obtain better student success for the same financial investment. I was unable to persuade the admissions and financial aid leadership to try a version of such a "moneyball" approach. I wasn't a profile in courage, as I didn't force them to do something. And then, not long afterwards, I fired the admissions and financial aid leadership because of over-awarding financial aid beyond approved parameters and didn't ever get to explore the possibility with the new leadership. Given the post-pandemic reduction in reliance on standardized tests, there is a great opportunity for colleges to carefully analyze whether they are most effectively using their limited financial aid resources. I suspect, though, that many will continue to use a version of whatever they've been doing all along.

Why Do Small Changes Cause Such Big Problems?

The concept of elasticity has shown up several times already. There is an unfortunate irony about effectively operating a college. In chapter 5, we investigated tuition discounting as a form of price discrimination and saw that the key was that the marginal revenue from enrolling a student needed to be positive. Here's where elasticity comes in. In general, elasticity measures how responsive a decision is to a change in some feature—for example, how many additional students enroll if additional financial aid is awarded. If the responsiveness is high, we call the response "elastic," while if it is low, we call it "inelastic." For the marginal revenue to be positive, the response must be elastic. Intuitively, if the response is inelastic, then lowering the price (increasing financial aid) doesn't increase the number of students, so all we're doing is collecting less money from each student. For revenue to increase, we need enough new students to offset the decreased revenue per student.

The condition of being in an elastic response situation is an irony of operating efficiently. Generating surplus means setting a price where there will be a big response to any changes, because marginal revenue will be greater than or equal to marginal costs, which are greater than zero. That means that if we set the price just above or below the optimal level, we will see a big response. If we set the price too high, then we lose a lot of students. If we set the price too low, we enroll so many students that we must increase our costs, perhaps to the extent that our net revenues decrease.

The idea of high elasticity being optimal is not restricted to setting prices, though. It applies to any condition that a college can control, even something as seemingly evanescent as campus culture. Consider the experience of New College of Florida in 2023, after Governor DeSantis appointed a new set of trustees charged with making radical changes in the school, using Hillsdale College as the example toward which New College should aspire. One immediate impact was a substantial improvement in the fortunes of Hampshire College in Massachusetts, which was a comparable school in terms of its pedagogical approach. It is certainly the case that the new leadership at New College has taken a bold step away from the herd, and it remains to be seen whether there is a substantial influx of students excited about the new direction there. But even for people leading schools that are not in the national spotlight, choosing a new direction (or choosing to keep going in the same direction) is fraught with peril, because if you're doing things right, you're at the point where students are highly responsive at the margin to your changes. Living one semester away from a crisis is not only a feature of small college life. It is a feature of effective leadership of a small college.

To summarize, the optimal position for a college is to be in a situation where students' response at the margin to price is highly elastic while creating a unique campus culture and identity not easily copied. Easier said than done.

10

Regulation

Higher education in the United States is much more heterogeneous than in most other countries. At the same time, it is an incredibly regulated industry. There are unique features of the U.S. approach to regulating higher education, which raise some economic issues we've already seen (such as principal–agent problems) and some additional ones (especially the concept of regulatory capture). Some of the highest-profile issues affecting higher education in recent years, including Title IX and the response to COVID-19, include important regulatory dimensions.

Accreditation: Peer Review vs. Central Administration

In most countries, the ministry of education controls a relatively homogeneous set of higher educational institutions. While there might be varying degrees of institutional autonomy and student choice, the overall picture is of a common college experience. By contrast, the United States includes an incredible diversity of schools. They are large, small, public, private, narrowly focused on a single subject, or so broad as to include everything. Rather than take a "one size fits all" approach to regulating the schools, the

United States has historically chosen to empower a set of private institutions to establish whether a school qualifies for Federal financial aid for its students. These private institutions are called accreditors. These were originally voluntary associations of colleges that were trying to assure academic quality to potential students or theological orthodoxy to denominational sponsors, but they became part of the Federal regulatory apparatus with the explosive growth in government aid after World War II.

Because of the wide range of institutional missions and the heterogeneity of students served, accreditors do not simply impose a set of required outcomes. Instead, institutional accreditation focuses on the processes an institution follows toward achieving its mission. Special attention is paid to student outcomes: how they are defined, whether they are achieved, and whether there are processes in place to evaluate effectiveness and attempts to improve.

One feature of the regulatory regime has been the creation of a seamless transfer process across different states, because institutions in one state can be confident that institutions in other states have met similar accreditation standards. Among other interpretations, this reduces the downside risk of attending a school far from home, reflecting the bad news principle for making investments. In addition, the knowledge that a student can transfer if the first institution attended isn't the right fit provides further downside risk reduction. The recent moves by some states and perhaps the Federal government to reduce uniformity across jurisdictions run the risk of reducing clarity among students, colleges, and employers regarding the nature and quality of education obtained in different places.

The emphasis on process rather than outcomes is a source of frustration to many outside observers of higher education. After all, shouldn't people be aware of student outcomes before investing large amounts of money and time? This seems like the type of principal–agent problem we saw in chapter 2. The principal, in this case, is the potential student, and the agent is the college. (There is an additional principal–agent problem lurking here, with the principal being whoever is funding the student and the agent being the student who is expected to work hard.) This is the essential logic behind various types of "report cards" that have been proposed to provide a standard way to measure institutional outcomes. One of the most important, because of the author and its potential impact on public policy, is the College Scorecard (https://collegescorecard.ed.gov/) developed by the U.S. Department of Education.

There are several important difficulties in this approach. The first is that student outcomes are not entirely dependent on the work of the college. There is a strong correlation between family characteristics—especially education and income—and student graduation rates. A school that can attract students from better-educated and wealthier families will have better outcomes, even if its education is no better than another school with a less-advantaged student body.

A second difficulty is that different people are motivated by different things. Some people are looking to make a high salary and live in a large city, while other people are looking for a quiet life in a small town.

The third difficulty is that salaries by themselves do not measure quality of life. The cost of the house we own in suburban Cleveland is basically a down payment on a comparable house where our daughter lives in Boston, illustrating that the lifestyle available at a particular income level varies substantially from place to place.

Despite these difficulties, the effort in thinking through which outcomes matter and then finding common ways to provide information is a positive step toward helping people choose the institution that will serve them best. This is essentially an extension of the challenges we reviewed in chapters 8 and 9 regarding the effectiveness of rankings in providing useful information to potential students.

Accreditation can be viewed as a principal–agent situation, with the Federal government as the principal and the college as the agent. In terms of our overarching model of college governance, we can conceive of the Federal government (or state government) as having a preferred level of the characteristics of the school. In 2025, much of this dialogue has consisted of discussions about academic freedom and "wokeness," while previous years have included controversies about liberal arts versus vocational training, racial discrimination, and gender discrimination. The principal–agent view would describe accreditation as a monitoring approach to the question of whether the school is appropriately pursuing effective implementation of its unique mission for its students. The threat of withdrawing Federal financial aid, though, is such a massive penalty that it becomes usable only in the most extreme circumstances. The withdrawal of research grants in the early months of the second Trump administration, while targeted primarily at schools outside the scope of this book, are nevertheless relevant in signaling that extreme measures might be more common in the future than in the past.

Program Accreditation and Regulatory Capture

In addition to institutional accreditation, many academic disciplines and programs also operate an accreditation process. It is the same process of self-study followed by a peer review, only now focused on the individual program. Although each accreditor has its unique features, reflecting the history of the discipline and its current context, all of them share one important feature: they all serve as external lobbyists advocating for more resources to be devoted to their discipline.

In the economic analysis of regulation, there is a concept called regulatory capture. This is essentially an application of the logic of collective action, which we will discuss in more detail in chapter 11. The individuals and organizations being regulated have a strong incentive to control the regulatory body, because it will directly affect their situation. On the other hand, those who are being protected by the regulatory body typically do not have an easy way to work together. This is perhaps most easily seen in the case of future students, who are protected from subpar programs through the accreditation process but have no straightforward way of advocating for themselves as a group.

Ford Prefect—a fictional character in Douglas Adams's *Life, the Universe, and Everything* advocating apathy to his friends Arthur and Slartibartfast in the face of a powerful conqueror—illustrates the dilemma facing college leaders confronting the combined force of their own faculty and the external accreditor.

"The point is," he said, "that people like you and me, Slartibartfast, and Arthur—particularly and especially Arthur—are just dilettanti, eccentrics, layabouts if you like."

Slartibartfast frowned, partly in puzzlement and partly in umbrage. He started to speak. ". . . ." is as far as he got.

"We're not obsessed by anything, you see," insisted Ford.

". . ."

"And that's the deciding factor. We can't win against obsession. They care, we don't. They win" (Adams 1982, 107–108).

Lest this fictional example seem exaggerated, consider the example in 2024 of nursing at Dickinson State University. The president imposed a requirement that every full-time professor generate a minimum number of student credit hours (number of students multiplied by credit hours in the courses taught by the professor). These requirements were not attainable by nursing professors if they met the required student–faculty ratios needed to maintain accreditation. The entire nursing faculty resigned, precipitating a crisis that led shortly thereafter to the resignation of the president.[1]

Every discipline is a small world, and so people working within a discipline have an incentive to maintain good relations with their peers. The accreditation process typically assigns peer reviewers who truly come from comparable institutions, which reinforces this pattern. While I have no question about the integrity of the reviewers and have observed them making life uncomfortable for their colleagues during a site visit, there is nevertheless the incentive to be perceived as constructive. One way to do that is to repackage the list of improvements desired by the host institution's faculty as a set of recommendations from the accreditor. This increases the possibility that the improvements will be implemented and increase the prestige of the discipline while also maintaining goodwill with the host institution's faculty.

Although most institutions don't have a law school, the law school accrediting body displayed perhaps the best example of this phenomenon. There were maximum student–faculty ratios, maximum teaching loads, and requirements for faculty leave incorporated into the accreditation standards. And for many years, a requirement for being accredited was that the faculty salaries be higher than average. Although such an outcome might be feasible in Garrison Keiller's fictional Lake Wobegon, in practice it is impossible for every school to have above-average salaries. The result, then, was a ratchet effect where every year the law schools being accredited would increase their salaries to above average, which in turn raised the average facing the schools being accredited in the following years. Ultimately, the U.S. Department of Justice brought an antitrust action against the American Bar Association, leading to changes in the accreditation requirements.[2]

Teacher Certification as Regulatory Capture

A textbook case of regulatory capture is teacher certification. Research on teaching effectiveness has two broad conclusions. First, it is extremely difficult to predict who will be an effective teacher, and the best way to identify effective teachers is to observe them teaching for a few years. Second, the best preparation for a teacher is a strong undergraduate program in the discipline that they teach, combined with some basic classroom management skills and experience in classrooms. Instead, undergraduate students wishing to be certified to teach in public schools face a daunting set of course requirements that reduce time in their academic discipline. Even more challenging is that those requirements differ from state to state, and most states do not have reciprocal agreements regarding certification. To put it bluntly, if you don't go to college in the state where you want to work, you either must give up the possibility of teaching in public schools or face an arduous process of meeting the local requirements.

Who benefits from such a policy? The students? No, unless you believe that all the most effective teachers for a state happened to attend college in that state. Further, potential good teachers in the state might be discouraged by the arbitrary nature of some of the requirements and their narrow focus. Future teachers? No, because their geographical options have now been limited, even for those who have decided to go ahead. Current teachers? Yes, because they have reduced the potential competition, making it possible for them to either extract higher salaries or increase job security.

There are two other beneficiaries from ever-more restrictive policies regarding teacher certification. The first is elected officials, because campaigning on a platform of "improving the quality of teachers" is popular, and not much attention is paid to the actual impact of these policies. The second is state colleges and universities that grew out of the normal school/teacher's college tradition, as they reduce competition with private institutions that have more substantial core curriculums and academic disciplinary requirements.

As a final footnote regarding regulatory capture, consider the case of Florida's decision in 2022 to require its public colleges and universities to change their institutional accreditor every ten years.[3] A sympathetic view of this requirement is that it is an attempt to prevent the sort of friendly peer interactions that lead institutions to support each other through the process rather than acting on behalf of students. Similarly, some of the executive orders by the Trump administration in 2025 over topics such as DEI and critical race theory can be viewed through this lens as well. If in fact institutions are cooperating to advance policy views of their faculty and staff rather than acting on behalf of students, then external regulation might be needed to maintain balance. Introducing competition among accreditors, enacted under the first Trump administration in 2019, could also serve as a countervailing force to the formation of cartels that don't act in favor of students.

Antitrust Issues in Higher Education

Colleges both compete and cooperate with each other. An important dimension of government regulation is preventing the formation of monopolies or cartels and also regulating company behavior to prevent exploitation of consumers. Much of the media attention in higher education has been devoted to athletic issues, including whether athletes can be paid for participation in intercollegiate competition. This question is not salient for most small colleges, which in many cases are not offering athletic scholarships or attracting millions of dollars in media packaging. Similarly, the concerns about elite institutions coordinating financial offers to reduce the amount of aid available to students are not relevant to institutions that are engaged in tuition discounting to attract students.

There are antitrust issues that are directly related to the concerns of small colleges, though. One recent example was the decision to change the code of ethics required for participation in the National Association for College Admission Counseling, the main professional association for admissions professionals. Previously, colleges were constrained in their efforts to recruit students who had already committed to another school, which arguably reduced the ability of the students to obtain the largest amount of aid. There also used to be limits on the use of nonfinancial incentives to attract students. The changes to the ethics code in 2019 added new dimensions of competition in the form of incentives and outreach to students who had deposited elsewhere while also increasing the uncertainty facing tuition-driven institutions that now had another reason to be concerned about accurately predicting their enrollment in the coming year.[4]

Title IX

Ineffective regulation can hinder the achievement of laudable policy goals. Since its adoption in 1972, Title IX has fostered equal opportunity for women, which is a desirable outcome. But since 2011, it has become perhaps the leading example of how not to implement effective regulation. During that time, there have been a series of large changes in the requirements, some of which went through the official rulemaking process and some of which were requirements disguised as suggestions.

The high profile attached to these regulations dates to a "Dear Colleague" letter issued by the Office of Civil Rights in President Obama's Department of Education in April 2011. This letter explained that sexual violence is a form of sexual harassment and that colleges are therefore responsible for preventing and punishing it under Title IX. More controversially, it required schools to use a "preponderance of the evidence" standard for adjudicating cases. A follow-up guidance document issued in 2014 further detailed aspects of Title IX regulation that were required of colleges. Because the documents were guidance letters rather than rules adopted through the official process, schools were put in a difficult situation regarding compliance. The Department of Education claimed that it was only guidance while simultaneously attacking colleges that didn't adopt the guidance. When President Trump took office in 2017, the guidance was rescinded, and new rules were put into place. Rulemaking is a time-consuming process, so the new regulations were only in place a short while before President Biden took office, and the review and revision process began anew. New regulations took effect on August 1, 2024—except for the twenty-six states where injunctions prevented their implementation. Perhaps the only thing more complicated than the whipsawing of these regulations from administration to administration is compounding them with a state-by-state variation in whether the Federal regulations can be enforced. While there is no one (I hope!) who would object to the goal of removing barriers for all people to fully benefit from education, it is still reasonable to ask for consistency and predictability in implementing regulations that bring with them considerable costs.

One administrative challenge of the Title IX rules is that they prescribe a judicial process that is not compatible with other student offenses. This means that the adjudication of a case of intimate partner violence could be very different than the adjudication of a case of assault. In particular, there is at least implicitly a requirement for several attorneys to be involved in Title IX cases under the Trump administration rules. This is a substantial burden for small colleges, most of which do not employ a full-time attorney, much less several.

The other challenge with Title IX is that it can be used to preempt the process for determining capital projects and operating budgets. I am familiar with a situation in which members of an athletics team filed a Title IX complaint regarding their team's competition facility. That case remains officially on the books, long after the students graduated, even though the competition facility has benefited from major investments during the intervening years. I had the opportunity to meet the students who filed the complaint, and they sincerely thought they were doing the institution a favor by providing it with external pressure to undertake actions they believed were in its best interests.

Case Study: An Impossible Situation

An old joke about regulation explains that everything not compulsory is forbidden. This might seem to be an extreme version of constraint, as it does not allow any freedom of action. But in practice, regulations can be even more restrictive, leading to a situation where there is no way forward for a college without potential liability. Or, to put it succinctly: everything is forbidden, but the institution still must act. Consider the following example.

A student accused a professor of sexual harassment. Thus, we were investigating a Title IX case. However, that same student was also credibly believed to pose a potential threat to themselves or others. Typically, in such a situation, the student would be removed temporarily from the campus environment until the concern was resolved. However, given the accusation, such a move could be viewed as retaliation by the institution against the student.

Our college's attorney confirmed the dilemma. If we did not act, and the student harmed themself or others, then the college was liable for failing to take appropriate precautions. If we acted, then the college was liable to be accused of retaliation. No matter what, the college was at risk.

What would you do? Here's where thinking like an economist helped. The point is to choose the path with the highest net benefits. Given that no matter what we did, we faced uncertain costs, the key was to try and maximize the benefits. I asked the dean of students what she would recommend as best for the student and the college, putting the question of legal liability on one side. She responded that removing the student from campus was the right approach. And that's what we did. The student threatened to sue us for retaliation, and we wound up settling (paying a substantial amount of money) after a mediation process. We also pursued the Title IX case and parted ways with the faculty member as well.

COVID-19: Regulation

Perhaps the defining event of the past decade has been the COVID pandemic. It is hard to find a better example of uncertainty, in the sense proposed in chapter 8, instead of risk. There were many challenges to small colleges because of the pandemic, but my focus here is on the impact of regulation.

First, there were typically inconsistencies between the guidance coming from the Centers for Disease Control and Prevention or other Federal government sources and the regulations promulgated by state and local governments. In both Tennessee and South Carolina, where I was a president, the state governments worked to restrict the ability of local governments to impose mask mandates and the ability of employers (including educational institutions) to require vaccines. In other states, the policy initiatives were in the opposite direction. As a result, there were very different pandemics depending on where you lived. Consider one anecdote: the Council of Independent Colleges, the major trade group for small private colleges, annually conducts interviews with a sample of presidents. I was randomly selected to be interviewed in April 2021 by a staff member from Maryland (their offices are in Washington, DC). Her first question was when the faculty, staff, and students would return to campus. My answer was June 2020 for faculty and staff and August 2020 for students. She was flabbergasted, as she was still working remotely and had only made three trips to the office in the previous year to pick up or drop off materials.

Second, the cost of implementing regulations, whether government mandated or locally instituted, were considerable. The government aid packages helped in purchasing supplies but were temporary. Further, at least in South Carolina, there was substantial resistance to any mask, vaccine, or testing requirements. In addition to the financial burden, I had to choose how much political capital to spend arguing with faculty members convinced that ivermectin was an adequate substitute for vaccination or with faculty members who believed that we should continue cleaning classrooms after every class despite the evidence that surface transmission was so rare as to make this practice inefficient.

Exempt Salary Minimum

One challenge for leaders of small colleges is that much of the national discussion about higher education treats highly selective institutions as the norm rather than as an exception. In many cases, this is annoying rather than harmful. And, for many people in positions of influence and power, it is true that their experience and that of many of their professional acquaintances will have been at elite, highly selective institutions, so it is understandable why they might believe it is typical. The problem is when policy is made in the belief that a place like Harvard is representative, rather than the opposite.

The clearest example of national policy being set with a lack of appreciation for institutional heterogeneity is the recurring issue of the minimum salary threshold for exempt employees. This regulation is administered by the Department of Labor (DOL) and represents part of the test for whether an employee is exempt from being paid overtime or not. While not solely a higher education rule, it nevertheless has important consequences for colleges—particularly small colleges located away from coastal metropolitan areas.

In 2015, the Obama administration suggested increasing the minimum salary threshold from $23,660 (where it had been for several decades, so clearly it was overdue for a change) to $50,440, which was the 40th percentile for full-time salaried workers. The DOL also proposed indexing the threshold, so that it would change on an annual basis rather than needing to go through the rulemaking process each time. I thought that indexing made sense and agreed that increasing the threshold was a good idea. But the proposed increase was well outside of what Maryville College could have absorbed in a straightforward manner.

Because educators are not covered by the salary threshold, the regulation would not have directly changed what the school was required to pay faculty. However, it would have a substantial impact on staff. During the spring of 2016, as the increase in the threshold was being discussed, Maryville College (along with many other schools) calculated the impact of the increase, assuming that no duties were changed and no employees were reclassified from exempt to nonexempt (i.e., eligible for overtime pay). In April 2016, the college employed 150 exempt professional staff. A move to the $50,440 threshold would have affected one hundred employees, with a projected increase in salaries and benefits of $1.3 million. Alternatively, if those employees were reclassified to nonexempt, there would be overtime payments of between $621,000 and $1,862,000, depending on whether the average overtime was five hours per week or fifteen hours per week. To put these figures in context, the total salary and benefits for the entire college at the time was about $16 million.

In addition to the direct financial impact of the proposed change, there were other possible effects. First, to make the overtime affordable, we considered cutting regular hours to 37.5 or even 35, as overtime wages only apply above 40 hours per week. Second, there were three morale issues: employees who viewed being classified as exempt implying higher status than nonexempt and resenting reclassification; faculty paid below the threshold who were not guaranteed a raise; and employees in positions that are required to work 40 hours per week compared to those under 40 hours per week.

To the type of person occupying policymaking positions at the DOL and living in Washington, DC, a $50,000 salary probably sounded pretty low. But in the suburbs of Knoxville, Tennessee, $50,000 wasn't too bad. We had one small political advantage, in that the senator who chaired the relevant committee, Lamar Alexander, was born and raised in Maryville and was receptive to the arguments made by small colleges like ours. In the end, the threshold was increased to $35,568 (in 2019, after some more drama) but not indexed. Therefore, the next increase in the threshold had to go through a similar process, and in August 2023 the Biden administration started that process. The new rules increased the threshold to $43,888 on July 1, 2024, and $58,656 on January 1, 2025. Importantly, they also mandate an update every three years. While this means ongoing salary increases for colleges to fund, it also provides a measure of stability and predictability, which is a benefit.[5]

The Regressive Nature of Regulation

In economic jargon, a policy is regressive (progressive) if it places a higher (lower) burden on less well-off people than on well-off people. Although economists prefer to focus on individuals rather than institutions when assessing how regressive or progressive a policy is, I depart from strict analytical rigor in this instance for the sake of clarity. In addition to everything else that is problematic about government regulation, particularly at the national level, it is also typically regressive. The burden of complying with regulations is proportionately greater for small colleges than large colleges and for poor colleges relative to rich colleges.

Why is regulation regressive? Generally, it's because the cost of regulation is fixed. To think about it in a simple way, suppose that complying with a regulation means hiring one person at a cost of $60,000. If my college only employs one hundred people with a total payroll of $6 million, then that represents a 1 percent increase. On the other hand, if my college employs 1,000 people with a total payroll of $60 million, then the regulation represents a 0.1 percent increase. Although complying with regulations is typically more complicated than this simple example, the general point still holds. To the extent that a regulation is one size fits all, it will be a more comfortable fit the bigger and richer you are.

With the growth in regulation of online education, small colleges found themselves navigating rules in providing education that differ across states. An interstate voluntary agreement overseen by a national organization (called the National Council for State Authorization Reciprocity Agreement, or NC-SARA) set standards for postsecondary distance education. In 2022, the Federal government proposed changing the requirements for delivering distance education that removed the benefit of NC-SARA, instead requiring every college to comply with consumer protection laws in every state where its students are located. This would be straightforward for large national providers, such as Western Governor's University or Southern New Hampshire University, but a huge barrier for small colleges. The final rule promulgated in 2023 scaled this requirement back, but it is a nice example of how regulations can have different impacts depending on the scale of the organization.[6]

The value of the tax exemption for endowment or exemption from property tax is also skewed toward wealthy institutions. After all, if an asset isn't taxed, the more valuable the asset, the greater the amount of tax is forgone. Consider two colleges that each enroll 1,000 students. One of them has a physical plant valued at $100 million and an endowment worth $200 million that generates $10 million in income each year. The other school has a physical plant worth $50 million and an endowment worth $60 million that generates $3 million in income each year. If the property tax rate is 2 percent and the income tax rate is 25 percent, then the first college receives an implicit subsidy of $4.5 million: $2 million in property tax relief and $2.5 million in foregone income taxes on the endowment income. The second college receives only $1.75 million. For colleges and universities with huge endowments or valuable property, the implicit benefit per student can be much larger than the explicit subsidies provided to public colleges and universities.

Why Do So Many People Get College Degrees?

In higher education circles, the question that heads this section is nonsensical. After all, less than 40 percent of American adults have earned a bachelor's degree. And it is an article of faith that the main problem is increasing the number of students and helping them persist through graduation. After all, the average lifetime wage premium for a college graduate relative to someone who only completes high school is about $1 million. College graduates vote in higher proportions than other people. They are also disproportionately represented in a variety of community leadership positions. Surely the advantages of college are obvious.

There is another popular line of argument, however, advocating for fewer college students. (Fact: college enrollment has been decreasing for more than a decade, so perhaps this line of argument has more persuasive power than college leaders want to admit.) The most sophisticated version of this argument is that the average lifetime wage premium obscures a substantial amount of heterogeneity, making college a poor financial investment for many people. The least sophisticated version tells anecdotes of (insert your least favorite major here) graduates working as baristas or asking if you would like fries with that. Moreover, there are accusations that the college graduates are being indoctrinated to vote in particular ways by their professors, making their overrepresentation in community leadership a problem rather than a benefit.

One interesting dimension to the question of college attendance and graduation is the impact of regulation. In this case, the regulation has to do with equal employment opportunity. There was a time that employers could discriminate based on race. The 1964 Civil Rights Act prohibited that behavior. In an important case, *Griggs v. Duke Power* (1971), the Supreme Court found that aptitude tests that were not directly connected to job duties violated the Civil Rights Act. Prior to this case, many employers required college degrees as an indicator of readiness for employment. However, now the degree requirement must be directly tied to the ability to perform the work.

Nevertheless, possessing a college degree retains its importance as a credential for employment. One example I'm familiar with is Enterprise Car Rental, which heavily recruited for its management track among new bachelor's degree graduates. If the entry requirement for a professional position is a bachelor's degree, even if the degree isn't necessary, then all else being equal, more people will complete bachelor's degrees. In response to labor shortages and to a changing political environment, many states are removing degree requirements and emphasizing specific skills when hiring. Removing the "paper ceiling" for a wide range of jobs can serve as an additional structural challenge to the business model of enrollment-driven colleges.

11

Mergers, Consortia, Startups, and Closures

I was enjoying a conversation with a friend who is an investment banker. He questioned me about my work, encouraging me to describe the various challenges facing small colleges. He said that, in his world, an industry with many undercapitalized firms operating at an inefficiently small scale would be ripe for mergers and takeovers. Why don't we see mergers and takeovers happening on a large scale among small colleges? I thought it was an excellent question and told him that I didn't have a short answer. This is my attempt to provide a longer answer to my friend, as well as to others who might reasonably ask the same question.

Why Don't More Colleges Merge?

As with any good mystery, there are a variety of suspects, each of whom could plausibly be blamed. Let's review all of them and see where the explanation lies.

No Reward for Investors

In chapter 5, we saw that most colleges are organized as nonprofit organizations, and throughout the book we emphasized how this alters the bargaining power between donors and other stakeholders. How does this affect the case of mergers and acquisitions? A for-profit company has owners who benefit from the profits (surplus) the company creates, either because the value of their ownership stake (such as shares of stock) increases or because the profits are distributed as a dividend. A defining feature of a nonprofit is the non-distribution constraint, which forbids the financial surplus generated by the nonprofit from being distributed to individuals.

Merging colleges or acquiring colleges is difficult. In fact, changes in government regulation have made it even more difficult than it was just a couple of years ago when I was first asked this question by my friend. Typically, people want to be rewarded for undertaking difficult work. The nonprofit nature of colleges means that there are limited financial rewards to a person for engaging in the process. It also means that it isn't possible for an investor to purchase a college or colleges, improve their operations, and then sell them for a profit. While it is not true that everyone is motivated by money, it is true that the absence of financial rewards considerably attenuates the incentive to do this work.

Logic of Collective Action I: Diffuse Benefits

Improving the effectiveness of a college benefits many people. If one added up the value to all those people, then it would almost surely exceed whatever the costs are of making the improvements. When benefits exceed costs, it seems obvious that such a change would occur. But it is not so obvious once we consider that such a change requires many people to work together. An economist, Mancur Olson (1965), developed a theory about changes that provide net overall benefits but require collective action. He emphasizes that such a change is less likely if the benefits are diffuse across many people and if it is difficult for those people to cooperate.

Students, and especially future students, are each likely to gain from an improvement in college effectiveness and efficiency. But it is unlikely that a single student, or even a small group of students, will benefit enough for them to push through a merger. In the case of future students, cooperation is even more unlikely, as those students have no way to identify each other to communicate and work together.

What about faculty and staff members? The greater economic stability and perhaps the greater effectiveness of a merged college might seem appealing. But it isn't necessarily the case that the benefits at the institutional level translate directly into benefits at the individual level. If I enjoy teaching all my courses in person and a merger will mean that I must teach some of them online, then I might not be very happy, even if my salary increases and my employment stability is better. (This is another example of the tension between what faculty want and what students, administrators, and donors want.) And it is uncertain, at least in advance of the merger, if my salary will increase and my employment stability will improve. With uncertain benefits that will only accrue in the future, it might be challenging to convince me to take on any costs of helping to organize in favor of a merger or an acquisition. The bad news principle introduced in chapter 8 when analyzing decision-making under uncertainty is relevant here. It suggests that what is important to generate faculty and staff support (or at least reduce opposition) is reducing the potential negative consequences of a merger rather than increasing the potential positive effects.

Logic of Collective Action II: Concentrated Costs

The logic of collective action also applies when looking at how costs are distributed. In this case, it is more difficult to engage in collective action that provides a net benefit if the costs are concentrated and if those who incur the costs find it easy to cooperate. In the case of college mergers, both conditions apply.

It is usually not popular to publicly advocate for a merger, and it is never popular to advocate that one's institution gets acquired. (In 2022, we saw an exceptional case—Bloomington College in New Jersey openly asked for a merger partner and succeeded in attracting one.[1]) The focus of negative attention in these cases is the president, with the board of trustees usually being criticized as well. Clearly the president, as an individual, does not face a challenge in identifying the costs and having an incentive to reduce them. Similarly, the board is typically small relative to the number of current and potential students and even with respect to the number of faculty and staff. The board also does not face a challenge in organizing, as it already exists with a primary purpose of governance and strategic direction, making mergers and acquisitions part of its normal responsibilities.

While it is possible that the current faculty and staff could benefit from a merger, it is almost certain that the change will entail some costs. If nothing else, there is institutional change, and change always brings some costs. In the case of faculty and staff, one possible cost is a loss of autonomy if the college becomes part of a larger entity. Another potential cost is the potential loss of employment, which is at least implied by the superficially neutral phrase "increased efficiency." Even if my job duties stay the same, I might end up having to relocate if my department is moved elsewhere. Our overarching framework from chapter 1 suggests that faculty and staff might have a different preference than the board/administration as to what type of education is delivered and in what way. As we saw in chapter 7, the secular missionaries already have strong reasons to effectively use voice to oppose perceived institutional errors or deviations from their preferred approach. Thus, there are existing shared-governance mechanisms ready for use by those who want to mobilize opposition to a merger or acquisition. While it is true that those mechanisms are also available to mobilize in favor of a merger, the more uncertain and diffuse benefits to any given person make it less likely that such an outcome will occur.

Efficiency Benefits from Consortia

One advantage of merged institutions is the possible efficiencies gained from shared resources and greater purchasing power. There are a variety of state and national organizations that provide shared purchasing and other shared services to their members. It is possible that these consortia lessen the cost disadvantage for small colleges, reducing the potential benefit from a merger. To give just one example, the Appalachian College Association operates a library with a collection of ebooks and database subscriptions available to all its members, which are small private colleges in Appalachia. The extent of the collection and its cost are much more appealing than any of the schools could achieve on their own.

Similarly, on the academic front, there are consortia that allow students from one college to easily and seamlessly take advantage of course offerings elsewhere. Longstanding local partnerships include schools near Philadelphia (Haverford/Swarthmore/Bryn Mawr) and in Amherst, Massachusetts (where four colleges helped create Hampshire College to augment the educational ecosystem there). Successful regional academic partnerships include the Associated Colleges of the South and the Great Lakes Colleges Association. More recently, Acadeum has been a leader in building a network of online courses for schools looking to expand their opportunities in that growing dimension of education. This network has not only been independently developed by the firm, but it has simultaneously engaged other existing consortia as partners, building on the cooperative infrastructure already in existence. As we saw in chapter 2, it is much easier to cooperate on specific issues than it is to completely merge, and it is easier to build new partnerships when there is already an existing relationship of trust.

Mergers Happen, Just Not Quickly

By this point, you're likely convinced that it's not straightforward to consummate a merger or acquisition. However, difficult is not the same as impossible. There are mergers and other changes of control happening every year. Three that have attracted attention in the past few years are Boston College's acquisition of Pine Manor College, the partnership between Otterbein University and Antioch College, and Northeastern's acquisition of Mills College. In fact, there is a steady rhythm of such transactions, which over time translates to a significant change. A famous book by Astin and Lee profiling small colleges was published in 1971. Almost 50 years later, a journal article (Tarrant et al., 2018) described the then-current status of the 491 colleges studied in the book. While 354 of the schools continued to operate as private four-year institutions, 80 had closed and 57 had merged, been acquired, or converted to two-year schools.

I should probably disclose that I was a professor at a school that resulted from a merger in the 1960s, Case Western Reserve University. Coincidentally, given the civic rivalry between Cleveland and Pittsburgh, Carnegie-Mellon University was formed by a merger at about that same time.

It can also be the case that a merger is unwound. Columbia College (women) and Wofford College (men) in South Carolina were founded on the same day in 1854 by the Methodist Church. In the late 1940s, the schools were linked with the president of Wofford also taking charge of Columbia. However, that move was reversed after a few years. Even college closures can be reversed, as the example of Sweet Briar College illustrates.

Regulatory Hurdles

Higher education is a highly regulated industry, as discussed in chapter 10. One of the most important regulatory actors is the institutional accrediting body. Among other functions, these accreditors are the gatekeepers for eligibility for Federal financial aid, including both grants and subsidized student loans. The willingness of accreditors to look favorably on mergers and acquisitions has varied across space and time. No school will willingly risk its institutional accreditation, so the outlook of its accreditor will have a significant impact on the possibility of change of control.

Institutional accreditors, though, can also serve to promote transition. A school that is on the cusp of losing accreditation can be highly motivated to seek a partner. Unfortunately, the lags in the regulatory process mean that such a school might be unattractive as a partner by the time its peril is clear.

In 2023, the Department of Education changed its rules regarding approval of college mergers. Perhaps the most important change is that the department will only review a deal after the accreditor has approved it. And until the approval process is complete, the college must continue to operate as an independent institution. These changes were justified based on protecting students but have the effect of adding both uncertainty and time to any potential merger.[2] Financial distress can be a self-fulfilling prophecy as an institution moves from "one semester away from a crisis" into "crisis" due to falling enrollment.

Who Done It?

In the case of the missing mergers, like the case in *Murder on the Orient Express*, all the suspects contribute to the outcome. But the primary explanation, for me, is the nondistribution constraint. The reason this issue rises to the top is because of the clear contrast with the for-profit higher education environment. Mergers and acquisitions have been a prominent part of the landscape there, even though many of the other features of higher education remain similar to those of nonprofits. The for-profit schools have the same regulatory features, including institutional accreditation, and they hire from the same pool of educators. One reason that they engage in mergers or acquisitions is to improve efficiency, including achieving a scale that provides better purchasing power or brand recognition. Interestingly, well-known nonprofit institutions have been active in various ways in this for-profit area, with the Purdue acquisition of Kaplan as perhaps the exemplary case.

Why Nonprofit?

If the reason that colleges don't merge is the nondistribution constraint, then we are left with a further mystery. Why do nonprofit (and public) institutions dominate higher education, particularly in terms of prestige? After all, most of the U.S. economy consists of for-profit firms, so it can't be the case that the nonprofit corporate form is intrinsically superior. And consider that the nondistribution constraint almost guarantees that nonprofits will be undercapitalized, as there is no upside (capital gains) to someone who decides to invest, limiting the investors to people motivated by philanthropic or status reasons.

Burton Weisbrod (1988) identified situations where nonprofits can successfully compete with public-sector and for-profit institutions. One important example is in the case of experience goods, also known as trust goods, which are defined as goods whose quality cannot be determined until after one purchases or consumes them. As the name implies, the person purchasing a trust good is forced to believe that the seller of the good is being honest. The absence of a profit motive gives some assurance that the seller of the trust good is reliable, all else being equal.

Education is a quintessential example of a trust good. A person pays a substantial amount of money and invests a great deal of time and effort in return for the promise of both a positive experience while enrolled and a better life after graduation. Consider that one benefit of a liberal arts education is learning how to learn, which means that the investment in formal education pays dividends for years—even decades—after graduation. While this is true and a remarkable feature of higher education, it also means that people are paying considerable amounts today for a benefit that won't materialize for a long time. This is a situation rife with prospects for exploitation by unscrupulous operators.

Like other situations where there are large upfront costs, many people borrow money to pay for higher education. There is considerable media attention to this issue, and appropriately so given the scale of the total debt. What is less often emphasized, though, is that the bulk of the debt is not the result of borrowing by undergraduate students at nonprofit colleges and universities. Total borrowing by undergraduates, including those enrolled at community colleges and for-profit schools, only accounts for about half of the total debt. The remainder is borrowed by graduate and professional students. While some of this debt might be ill-advised, much of it reflects the lucrative professional prospects for graduates of, for example, medical specialty programs. What is especially interesting is that a higher fraction of for-profit students borrow than nonprofit students, and the average debt incurred by students at for-profit institutions is larger than at nonprofit institutions, despite a lower success rate. While not dispositive, this evidence is at least suggestive of nonprofits being truly focused on the welfare of their students as compared to for-profits.

What Changed?

As a bit of a coda, consider some high-profile examples drawn from the late 1800s and early 1900s. There are multiple examples of "takeovers" and "startups" that remain prominent today. In terms of takeovers, Rockefeller's decision to invest a fortune in a small Baptist school (University of Chicago) and Duke's investment in a small Methodist college (Trinity College in Durham, North Carolina, now Duke University) provide a potential road map for today's tycoons. Startups include Stanford University and Rice University, both of which reflect their founder in their names. A more recent example of a major infusion of cash, while not really a takeover, is the Wallace estate at Macalester. Olin College of Engineering is an interesting example of a relatively recent startup.

It is still financially feasible for a wealthy individual to fundamentally transform a college. Every year, there are multiple gifts of more than $100 million, including in some years gifts of more than $1 billion. Typically, those gifts go to a predictable small group of universities, with Harvard, Johns Hopkins, and Stanford leading the list. While no doubt these investments are useful, they are not transformational.

Compare, though, what a $100 million investment could do at a small college. Consider a college with an enrollment of about 1,500, an annual operating budget net of financial aid of about $25 million, a physical plant worth (net of depreciation) of about $25 million, and an endowment of about $25 million (or, as I would describe it, Columbia College in 2022). The school could take half of the money—$50 million—and substantially revamp its physical plant. It could put the other half—$50 million—into its endowment, which at a 5 percent spend rate would yield $2.5 million per year. That would be a 10 percent increase in available revenue, which could underwrite important investments in personnel and programs.

Why don't wealthy individuals invest in this way? The short answer is, I don't know because I'm not that wealthy. The example of Mackenzie Scott, who is making substantial unrestricted cash gifts to undercapitalized nonprofits including colleges, demonstrates the level of impact possible. But she doesn't have many predecessors, and at least so far, she doesn't seem to have inspired many followers. This leads to my slightly longer answer, which draws on the analysis of donor motivation presented in chapter 3. Higher education, and giving to charitable causes, is inextricably related to status. The "Varsity Blues" cases illustrated how much parents were willing to pay to get their children enrolled in prestigious universities. And having one's name affiliated with Harvard or Stanford can garner more praise in elite circles than transforming the educational experience for hundreds of students at a less well-known institution. Thorstein Veblen (1899 [2015]) devoted an entire book to analyzing this impulse to try to impress others and describing its consequences. Interestingly, he went on to write another book while serving on the faculty of Stanford, critical of the way that higher education was diverted from its best impulses by the combination of pandering to students and the need to generate philanthropic contributions. He published that book in 1918, illustrating that while the current manifestations of the issues are new, the challenge to colleges is perennial.

Why Don't More Small Colleges Start?

It is an article of faith among the leadership, faculty, staff, and alumni of small colleges that they are superior to larger institutions. There are also three relevant empirical observations. First, small colleges are not evenly distributed across the country; they are concentrated in a band from New England through the Mid-Atlantic to the Midwest but are underrepresented in the Southeast and the West. Second, most students do not travel very far to attend school. For most colleges, the overwhelming majority of students live within a five-hour driving radius of campus—a one-day roundtrip from home. Third, the main areas of population growth are in the Southeast and the West.

Given the three empirical observations, one would expect that small colleges would be starting in the rapidly growing parts of the country. In the thirty years from 1993 to 2022, Florida grew from 13.7 million people to 22.2 million people. This increase of over 8 million people is approximately two-thirds the population of Pennsylvania, which has about ninety small colleges. On that basis, we might expect dozens of new private colleges to open in Florida. However, the number of new small colleges that have opened in Florida in the past three decades is zero. Instead, what we have seen is the ongoing expansion of public universities and community colleges. A similar pattern is seen in Texas, another state with a booming population. My experience as a small college president in Tennessee and South Carolina, two more states with growing populations, is that it is difficult to recruit students to this presumably better education, much less create a new institution. And I am not alone. The challenge is best summarized in my conversation with the president of Mills College several years before it merged with Northeastern. Mills is located a few miles from the University of California, Berkeley, and the president observed that they struggle to recruit a few hundred students while the university turns away thousands of well-qualified students. During my time in Tennessee, one small college, Martin Methodist, was acquired by the University of Tennessee as a branch campus, while another, Lambuth, closed and subsequently was acquired by the University of Memphis to serve as a branch campus.

There are several explanations for this seemingly anomalous outcome. One explanation has to do with the greater amenities to be enjoyed at large institutions. Football, fraternities and sororities, and other nonacademic benefits entice unwitting students, in this telling. Further, state subsidies that provide both operating and capital support make it financially difficult for enrollment-driven colleges to compete. The decline of the primary and secondary education system, too, is blamed for creating students who are more interested in partying than in studying. Naturally, these are the sort of explanations that are preferred by alumni and employees of small colleges.

An alternative explanation emphasizes the way that large universities have adapted many of the features of small colleges. These include organizing campuses into more navigable communities, increasing individualized advising and other student support services, and creating intimate academic experiences beyond the proverbial huge lecture hall. In this telling, universities now provide the best of both worlds, with the benefits of large-scale in reducing costs and creating options combined with the individual experience of a personalized setting. Naturally, these are the sorts of explanations preferred by alumni and employees of large universities.

So which story is correct? Well, the answer to every question posed by an economist is, "It depends." But regardless of which story one believes, it seems clear that the age of creating many small colleges is past.

Why Don't More Small Colleges Close?

Every year, about a dozen small colleges close. And every year, the prediction is made that a major wave of college closures is impending. My favorite is from the early 1980s, and I'm bringing it back again from chapter 1: "A specter is haunting higher education: the specter of decline and bankruptcy. Experts predict that between 10 percent and 30 percent of America's 3,100 colleges and universities will close their doors or merge with other institutions by 1995" (Keller 1983, 3). The apocalypse continues to be deferred, as discussed for example in Marcy (2023) or Gardner (2023).

A cynical description of economists is that we are "people who see something working in practice and ask whether it will work in theory." Guilty. What is a theoretical explanation for the persistence of small colleges?

The model we have used throughout the book provides insight into both why colleges stay open and how they might evolve because of enrollment and financial difficulties. If a for-profit corporation is making losses, it is going to face unhappy shareholders, and it might face the possibility of a takeover by a more successful firm. Neither of those disciplinary devices apply to nonprofit colleges. A college can stay open as long as it maintains enough liquidity to do so. In rare circumstances, this can mean attracting donations that permit business as usual to continue. But for most small colleges, maintaining liquidity means enrolling enough students to pay the costs to stay open. In terms of the model, this means that the students' power to determine the approach to education is increased at the expense of the faculty/staff and the administration/board. Broadly speaking, faculty believe in the value of a liberal arts education while students want a clear path to a job and career. The evolution of small college curricula, and even more the evolution of small college marketing, has been in the direction preferred by students.

Why will students enroll in a college that is struggling? There are three reasons. First, if the school closes, where would the students who would have enrolled go? There is limited geographic mobility of students, which implies that enough enrollment to pay variable costs might be maintained for a long time if there aren't too many local educational alternatives. The increased academic quality and selectivity of flagship public universities generate increased potential enrollment for small colleges by creating a cohort of good students unable to get accepted at their home state's university. Eventually deferred maintenance catches up, but that "eventually" can last a while.

Second, there is typically limited knowledge regarding small college financial situations.[3] Sometimes this reflects a deliberate choice by the administration to obscure or downplay difficulties. Sometimes it reflects a lack of understanding by the administration of the degree of difficulty it faces. I have been shocked to hear leaders of college boards talk about how they essentially sleepwalked into unsustainable debt and other financial crises. Regardless of the reason, students can have a difficult time distinguishing between a college that is financially robust and one that is on the brink. After all, for almost every college, an academic year or two with a substantial enrollment decrease could put them out of business, so robustness and frailty are truly relative terms.

Third, nonprofits (including small colleges) can often mobilize enough philanthropic support to pay some operating costs for a while, even if they can't generate enough to build a balance sheet that allows them to thrive. If a college falls into hard times, it can usually find enough friends to pass the hat to pay the electric bill. To be sustainable, what it needs is to build an endowment whose draw covers the electric bill, but that is not a short-run proposition.

Conclusion

As is common for people in leadership roles, I chaired my share of meetings. I regularly adjourned them by saying, "Arise, go forth and conquer." This is a line from Tennyson's epic poem, *Idylls of the King*, that I found helpful in keeping my own (and I hope others') spirits high as we pursued our work. But there is an ironic subtext to that line, as it is spoken to King Arthur as he prepares for the final battle that will end his kingship, although not his glory. This leads to another quote from that same poem that I often referred to as well: "The old order changeth, yielding place to new, And God fulfills himself in many ways, Lest one good custom should corrupt the world." I believe that small colleges are not only part of the old order but also part of the new. But just as has been true throughout their existence, they must find new ways of fulfilling their missions.

If you laid all the economists in the world end to end, they would never reach a conclusion. That's one of my favorite economist jokes, in part because it has multiple punchlines. (The others are, "They would all point in different directions" and, more darkly, "It would be a good thing.") If you've read this far, then you are unlikely to be surprised at my conclusion. I am not going to give you some sort of clickbait "10 tips for a successful small college based on economic theory," a common ending for a book of this sort. Instead, I will wish you much success in discerning the best possible way forward given the serious constraints under which you labor. Your college's situation is precarious—one semester away from a crisis—just as it always has been and will continue to be for the foreseeable future. But your college plays a vital role in the heterogeneous system of higher education in the United States that serves the full range of students better than any other country in the world. By giving of your limited time to learn about economic ideas, may you be more than repaid in ideas about how to better lead your school.

Further Reading

> Of anything beyond these, my child, beware. Of making many books there is no end, and much study is a weariness of the flesh.
>
> —Ecclesiastes 12:12

If you enjoyed reading this book—or even if you didn't but you think the subject is important—then there are many other resources available. To keep the length of the book manageable, I focused on a subset of economic topics and on a subset of college leadership questions. The choices reflected my personal experiences, which will not be identical to yours. Here are a few books that you might find helpful as you continue to learn more. I provide a short synopsis for each one along with ways in which it is different from mine.

Campus Economics: How Economic Thinking Can Help Improve College and University Decisions by Sandy Baum and Michael McPherson (2023, Princeton University Press)

Baum and McPherson introduce basic principles of economic analysis and demonstrate how they can be applied to analyzing colleges and universities. Like them, I use economic ideas to better understand the situations that schools face. However, my focus is on small, enrollment-driven institutions, while they cover the entire spectrum of postsecondary education, including community colleges, flagship public universities, and research universities. Also, their analysis is limited to the type of topics usually covered in a principles course; at times it is almost like reading an introductory textbook. I introduce a range of more advanced concepts in an accessible manner, letting the important questions facing small colleges drive which economic ideas are applied.

Demographics and the Demand for Higher Education by Nathan D. Grawe (2018, Johns Hopkins University Press)

The Agile College: How Institutions Successfully Navigate Demographic Change by Nathan D. Grawe (2021, Johns Hopkins University Press)

Grawe uses economic analysis to highlight an important part of the strategic landscape for higher education. His approach is to go deeply into one dimension of analysis, the evolving demographics of potential college-goers. He uses this deep dive to address the broad scope of higher education, including community colleges and large public universities. My approach is to focus on a narrower set of institutions, while using a broad scope of economic ideas to understand their situation. All economics involves tradeoffs—in this case between breadth and depth, and so our approaches are complementary.

How to Run a College: A Practical Guide for Trustees, Faculty, Administrators, and Policymakers by Brian C. Mitchell and W. Joseph King (2018, Johns Hopkins University Press)

Leadership Matters: Confronting the Hard Choices Facing Higher Education by Brian C. Mitchell and W. Joseph King (2022, Johns Hopkins University Press)

Mitchell and King use their experience to provide general advice on best practices in college leadership. Their focus is less on providing an analytical underpinning and more on providing specific suggestions for actions that will improve colleges. I see my work as complementary to theirs. Economic analysis provides a lens for better understanding the current status and prospects for a college, which in turn helps college leaders develop and apply the type of solutions that Mitchell and King recommend.

Cautionary Tales: Strategy Lessons from Struggling Colleges by Alice Brown (2012, Stylus Publishing)

Like Brown, my focus is on small schools and how best to lead them. Her case study approach is powerful in showing the ways that specific context matters. My approach draws on my personal experience leading the type of school that Brown describes while providing a broader analytical framework that can help leaders better understand their unique situations.

Colleges on the Brink: The Case for Financial Exigency by Charles M. Ambrose and Michael T. Nietzel (2023, Rowman & Littlefield)

This book provides specific tools for schools that are experiencing financial crises. The authors pay attention to both public and private institutions of various sizes and economic models, which share the common feature that only emergency measures will save them. My book is targeted at leaders of institutions that are at risk of winding up in situations where they will need this book to extricate themselves.

Winnebagos on Wednesdays: How Visionary Leadership Can Transform Higher Education by Scott Cowen with Betsy Seifter (2018, Princeton University Press)

This is in some ways the most similar approach to my book. Cowen draws on his extensive experience as a management school dean and university president, combining it with his academic and consulting expertise in organizational management to provide theoretically grounded practical wisdom. His academic expertise and his institutional focus are different from mine, but both of our books aim at a serious praxis with experience and theory as coequal drivers. (Full disclosure: from 1990 to 1998, Scott was dean of the management school where I was a professor.)

Unequal Colleges in the Age of Disparity by Charles T. Clotfelter (2017, Belknap Press)

Clotfelter is an accomplished economist who also served with distinction as a university administrator. This book considers the evolving impact of college education on disparities among individuals. He argues that one reason for increased inequality among individuals is the increased inequality among colleges and universities. The "one semester away from a crisis" schools are typically on the wrong side of this increase in inequality, while they typically serve a population most in need of college to reduce disparities. This book provides a sobering look at the environment in which small colleges operate.

The College Stress Test: Tracking Institutional Futures across a Crowded Market by Robert Zemsky, Susan Shaman, and Susan Campbell Baldridge (2020, Johns Hopkins University Press)

Zemsky et al. analyze the question of which colleges and universities are most at risk of closing. Unlike some of the dramatic media coverage of this topic, they are clear about how they come to their conclusions and measured in how they describe possible outcomes. While my analysis presumes that all colleges are somewhat at risk, Zemsky et al. quantify which places are most at risk and why.

Higher Education Accountability by Robert Kelchen (2018, Johns Hopkins University Press)

I provide one chapter that skims the ways in which colleges are accountable to introduce economic concepts related to regulation. Kelchen carefully documents the multiple actors in this dimension, including the Federal government, state governments, accreditors, and others. He helpfully provides geographical breadth and historical context for the current and likely future controversies.

Economics for Nonprofit Managers and Social Entrepreneurs by Dennis R. Young, Richard Steinberg, Rosemarie Emanuele, and Walter O. Simmons (2019, Edward Elgar Publishing)

This is exactly what it sounds like—a textbook presentation of important economic concepts for people managing nonprofit organizations. It is a wonderful resource for those who wish to dive deeper into economic ideas while remaining focused on those that are most relevant to leading small colleges.

Acknowledgments

This book is the result of more than two decades in leadership positions. I have accumulated more debts than can be recounted here and am grateful to all the faculty, staff, students, board members, volunteers, and peers who have supported and challenged me through the years. I will single out a few people for specific praise at the risk of neglecting others who are deserving.

Andrew Medvedev asked the question about college mergers that prompted much of chapter 11. He also hired me as a visiting professor at the Weatherhead School of Management at Case Western Reserve University from July 2023 through December 2024, which gave me time to complete the first draft of the book.

John Clark, the founder of Vienna Coffee, is an incredible community leader who provided me with the metaphor that led to the title of the book.

Peggy Solic at Rutgers University Press was an enthusiastic supporter of the book from the first time I told her about it. It's a lot easier to finish the book when the editor is telling you it's worth finishing.

The production teams at Rutgers University Press and Westchester Publishing Services have been wonderful to work with as they performed the many tasks that transform a raw document into a professionally produced book. I am grateful to Robie Grant for building the index.

Two people had a huge impact on my approach to leadership, although both of them died before I became a president. Richard Shatten provided an example of leadership that emphasized making the world a better place rather than impressing other people. David Bradford modeled how to infuse economic analysis into discussions with people who are not economists.

Anonymous reviewers provided constructive and creative suggestions that improved the book.

Kris Barnett, Dan Klingensmith, Sue Rivera, Beth Rushing, and Dennis Young generously gave their time to read draft versions of the manuscript and provided helpful comments.

My most important debt is to my family. The book is dedicated to my wife, Mary. Her love and support for more than 33 years has made everything possible. Our daughter, Beth, is a continual source of joy.

Notes

Chapter 4 Portfolio

1 The study and detailed data are found at National Association of College and University Business Officers (2024).
2 The discussion in this section is based on Schelling (1978), especially chapter 2.

Chapter 5 Making a Profit

1 Burd (2024) is a good introduction to this industry.
2 A good contemporaneous description is found in Jaschik (2015).

Chapter 7 Secular Missionaries

1 Maryville College historical information from Blair and Walker (1994). Modern information from National Center for Education Statistics (n.d.).
2 The analysis of differences in the impact of family across disciplines is from Schultz and Stansberry (2022). An interesting article about how people with access to elite institutions perpetuate this status in the economics profession is Gluckman and Diep (2023).
3 A description of the events is found in Wingfield (2023).

Chapter 9 Herding

1 The announcement is found in U.S. News & World Report (2023). Drozdowski (2023) provides some analysis of the likely outcomes.
2 Diep (2023) reports the story.

Chapter 10 Regulation

1 Coverage can be found in Zahneis (2024) or Palmer (2024).
2 The complete case history can be found in Antitrust Division (n.d.).
3 A summary of the requirement is in Schwartz (2022).
4 A recent article covering several antitrust issues is Kelderman (2025).
5 Coverage can be found in Blake (2024).
6 Coverage can be found in Knott (2023a).

Chapter 11 Mergers, Consortia, Startups, and Closures

1 Coverage can be found in Heyboer (2022).
2 Coverage can be found in Knott (2023b).
3 Carlson (2024) discusses this issue.

References

Adams, Douglas. (1982). *Life, the Universe, and Everything.* New York: Pocket Books.

Akerlof, George. (1984). *An Economic Theorist's Book of Tales.* New York: Cambridge University Press.

Antitrust Division, U.S. Department of Justice. (n.d.). *U.S. v American Bar Association.* Accessed September 6, 2024. https://www.justice.gov/atr/case/us-v-american-bar-association.

Astin, Alexander W., and Calvin B. T. Lee. (1971). *The Invisible Colleges: A Profile of Small, Private Colleges with Limited Resources.* New York: McGraw-Hill.

Avery, Christopher N., Mark E. Glickman, Caroline M. Hoxby, and Andrew Metrick. (2013). "A Revealed Preference Ranking of U.S. Colleges and Universities." *Quarterly Journal of Economics* 128(1):425–467.

Barzun, Jacques. (1968). *The American University: How It Runs, Where It Is Going.* New York: Harper & Row.

Baum, L. Frank. (1900 [1979]). *The Wizard of Oz.* New York: Ballantine Books.

Bernanke, Ben S. (1983). "Irreversibility, Uncertainty, and Cyclical Investment." *Quarterly Journal of Economics* 98(1): 85–106.

Bettinger, Eric P., Brent J. Evans, and Devin G. Pope. (2013). "Improving College Performance and Retention the Easy Way: Unpacking the ACT Exam." *American Economic Journal: Economic Policy* 5(2):26–52.

Bierce, Ambrose. (1906 [1958]). *The Devil's Dictionary.* New York: Dover Publications.

Blair, Carolyn L., and Arda S. Walker. (1994). *By Faith Endowed: The Story of Maryville College 1819–1994.* Maryville, TN: Maryville College Press.

Blake, Jessica. (2024). "Biden Administration Finalizes Overtime Rule." *Inside Higher Ed,* April 24, 2024. Accessed September 6, 2024.

https://www.insidehighered.com/news/government/2024/04/24/federal-overtime-rule-will-force-raises-some-college-employees.

Brandenburger, Adam, and Barry Nalebuff. (2021). "The Rules of Co-opetition." *Harvard Business Review*, January–February 2021. Accessed September 5, 2024. https://hbr.org/2021/01/the-rules-of-co-opetition.

Brooks, David. (2000). *Bobos in Paradise: The New Upper Class and How They Got There*. New York: Simon & Schuster.

Buckley, William F. (1952 [2002]). *God and Man at Yale: The Superstitions of "Academic Freedom"* (Fiftieth Anniversary Edition). Washington, DC: Regnery Publishing.

Burd, Stephen. (2024). "The Dark Art of Enrollment Management." *Chronicle of Higher Education*, May 23, 2024. Accessed April 16, 2025. https://www.chronicle.com/article/the-dark-art-of-enrollment-management?utm_source=Iterable&utm_medium=email&utm_campaign=campaign_13103383_nl_Academe-Today_date_20250403.

Burke, Edmund. (1790 [2009]). *Reflections on the Revolution in France*. New York: Oxford University Press.

Burland, Elizabeth, Susan Dynarski, Katherine Michelmore, Stephanie Owen, and Shwetha Raghuraman. (2023). "The Power of Certainty: Experimental Evidence on the Effective Design of Free Tuition Programs." *AER: Insights* 5(3):293–310. Accessed September 6, 2024. https://pubs.aeaweb.org/doi/pdfplus/10.1257/aeri.20220094.

Caldwell, Ian, and Dustin Thomason. (2004). *The Rule of Four*. New York: Bantam Dell.

Carlson, Scott. (2024). "Why It Can Be So Difficult to Gauge a College's Financial Health." *Chronicle of Higher Education*, March 8, 2024. Accessed September 6, 2024. https://www.chronicle.com/article/why-it-can-be-so-difficult-to-gauge-a-colleges-financial-health.

Case Western Reserve University. (2023). "Operating Budget: Fiscal Year 2024." Accessed September 5, 2024. https://case.edu/finance/sites/default/files/2023-08/2024%20Operating%20Budget%20Book.pdf.

Cassar, Lea, and Stephan Meier. (2018). "Nonmonetary Incentives and the Implications of Work as a Source of Meaning." *Journal of Economic Perspectives* 32(3):215–238.

Chetty, Raj, Matthew O. Jackson, Theresa Kuchler, Johannes Stroebel, Nathaniel Hendren, Robert B. Fluegge, Sara Gong, Federico González, Armelle Grondin, Matthew Jacob, Drew Johnston, Martin Koenen, Eduardo Laguna-Muggenburg, Florian Mudekereza, Tom Rutter, Nicolaj Thor, Wilbur Townsend, Ruby Zhang, Mike Bailey, Pablo Barberá, Monica Bhole, and Nils Wernerfelt. (2022). "Social Capital I: Measurement and Associations with Economic Mobility." Working Paper 30313. Cambridge, MA: National Bureau of Economic Research.

Chinman, Luke, and Izzy Polanco. (2023). "The College's 2024 Fiscal Year Budget, Explained." *The Williams Record*, July 1, 2023. Accessed

September 5, 2024. https://williamsrecord.com/464356/news/williams-college-budget-fiscal-year-2024-explained-fy24/#:~:text=The%20 2024%20fiscal%20year%20budget%20includes%20%24292%20 million,a%202.7-percent%20increase%20from%20the%202023%20 fiscal%20year.

Cleary, Thomas, editor and translator. (1990). *The Tao of Politics: Lessons of the Masters of Huainan* (Translations from the Taoist classic *Huainanzi*). Boston: Shambhala Publications.

Clotfelter, Charles T. (2017). *Unequal Colleges in the Age of Disparity*. Cambridge, MA: Belknap Press.

Dickson, Gordon. (1972). *Tactics of Mistake*. New York: DAW Books, Inc.

Diep, Francie. (2023). "This Year, One Major College Ranker Is Turning from Rankings to Ratings." *Chronicle of Higher Education*, June 22, 2023. Accessed September 6, 2024. https://www.chronicle.com/article/this-year-one-major-college-ranker-is-turning-from-rankings-to-ratings?utm_source=Iterable&utm_medium=email&utm_campaign=campaign_7101481_nl_Daily-Briefing_date_20230622&cid=db&source=ams&sourceid=.

Dolezal, Joshua. (2022). "The Big Quit: Even Tenure-line Professors Are Leaving Academe." *Chronicle of Higher Education*, May 27, 2022. Accessed September 5, 2024. https://www.chronicle.com/article/the-big-quit.

Drozdowski, Mark J. (2023). "U.S. News Adjusts Rankings Methodology, Emphasizes Diversity." *Best Colleges*, June 2, 2023. Accessed September 6, 2024. https://www.bestcolleges.com/news/analysis/us-news-adjusts-rankings-methodology-emphasizing-diversity/#:~:text=U.S.%20 News%20%26%20World%20Report%20announced%20changes%20 to,News%2C%20though%20the%20undergraduate%20rankings%20 remain%20largely%20unaffected.

Elias, Jacquelyn. (2024). "Who Does Your College Think Its Peers Are?" *Chronicle of Higher Education*, May 16, 2024. Accessed September 6, 2024. https://www.chronicle.com/article/who-does-your-college-think-its-peers-are.

Field, Kelly. (2024). "Ban on Transcript Holds Will Help Students, but Make It Harder for Colleges to Collect on Debt." *Chronicle of Higher Education*, April 10, 2024. Accessed September 5, 2024. https://www.chronicle.com/article/ban-on-transcript-holds-will-help-students-but-make-it-harder-for-colleges-to-collect-on-debt?utm_source=Iterable&utm_medium=email&utm_campaign=campaign_9541973_nl_Afternoon-Update_date_20240410&cid=pm&source=ams&sourceid=.

Fitzgerald, F. Scott. (1925). *The Great Gatsby*. New York: Collier Books.

Gardner, Lee. (2023). "When It Comes to College Closures, the Sky Is Never Going to Fall." *Chronicle of Higher Education*, March 24, 2023.

Accessed September 6, 2024. https://www.chronicle.com/article/when-it-comes-to-college-closures-the-sky-is-never-going-to-fall.

Glaeser, Edward. (2002). "The Governance of Not-For-Profit Firms." Working Paper 8921. Cambridge, MA: National Bureau of Economic Research.

Gluckman, Nell, and Francie Diep. (2023). "Does Raj Chetty Practice What He Preaches?" *Chronicle of Higher Education*, December 20, 2023. Accessed September 5, 2024. https://www.chronicle.com/article/does-raj-chetty-practice-what-he-preaches.

Gneezy, Uri, Stephan Meier, and Pedro Rey-Biel. (2011). "When and Why Incentives (Don't) Work to Modify Behavior." *Journal of Economic Perspectives* 25(4) 191–210.

Gneezy, Uri, and Aldo Rustichini. (2000). "A Fine Is a Price." *Journal of Legal Studies* 29(1) 1–17.

Grawe, Nathan. (2018). *Demographics and the Demand for Higher Education*. Baltimore, MD: Johns Hopkins University Press.

Heggen, Thomas. (1946 [1966]). *Mr. Roberts*. New York: Bantam Books.

Hirschman, Albert O. (1970). *Exit, Voice, and Loyalty: Responses to Decline in Firms, Organizations, and States*. Cambridge, MA: Harvard University Press.

Herbert, Frank. (1965). *Dune*. New York: Ace Books.

Heyboer, Kelly. (2022). "N.J. University Steps In to Save Bloomfield College from Shutting Down." *NJ.com,* March 23, 2022. Accessed September 6, 2024. https://www.nj.com/education/2022/03/nj-university-steps-in-to-save-bloomfield-college-from-shutting-down.html.

Jaschik, Scott. (2015). "Shocking Decision at Sweet Briar." *Inside Higher Ed*, March 3, 2015. Accessed September 4, 2024. https://www.insidehighered.com/news/2015/03/04/sweet-briar-college-will-shut-down.

J. P. Morgan Asset Management. (2024). *Guide to Retirement*. Accessed September 4, 2024. https://am.jpmorgan.com/us/en/asset-management/adv/insights/retirement-insights/guide-to-retirement/.

June, Audrey Williams. (2022). "'An Art and a Science': Colleges' Tricky Task of Selecting Peers." *Chronicle of Higher Education*, March 24, 2022. Accessed September 6, 2024. https://www.chronicle.com/article/an-art-and-a-science-colleges-tricky-task-of-selecting-peers.

Kelderman, Eric. (2022). "Confirming Faculty Fears, Purdue's Board Chair Says Trustees Chose President Like a Business." *Chronicle of Higher Education*, June 17, 2022. Accessed September 5, 2024. https://www.chronicle.com/article/confirming-faculty-fears-purdues-board-chair-says-trustees-chose-president-like-a-business.

Kelderman, Eric. (2025). "The Antitrust Attack." *Chronicle of Higher Education*, March 7, 2025. Accessed April 10, 2025. https://www.chronicle.com/article/the-antitrust-attack?utm_source=Iterable&utm

_medium=email&utm_campaign=campaign_13079064_nl_Academe-Today_date_20250401&sra=true.

Keller, George. (1983). *Academic Strategy: The Management Revolution in American Higher Education*. Baltimore, MD: Johns Hopkins University Press.

Knight, Frank H. (1921). *Risk, Uncertainty, and Profit*. New York: Houghton, Mifflin Company.

Knott, Katherine. (2023a). "A 'More Rigorous Process' to Determine Financial Aid Eligibility." *Inside Higher Ed*, June 2, 2023. Accessed September 6, 2024. https://www.insidehighered.com/news/government/student-aid-policy/2023/06/02/education-department-rethinks-financial-aid?utm_source=Inside+Higher+Ed&utm_campaign=1a4d68effd-DNU_2021_COPY_02&utm_medium=email&utm_term=0_1fcbc04421-1a4d68effd-236544006&mc_cid=1a4d68effd&mc_eid=8f99cd18b6.

Knott, Katherine. (2023b). "Feds Complicate College Mergers, With Possible Unintended Consequences." *Inside Higher Ed*, August 21, 2023. Accessed September 6, 2024. https://www.insidehighered.com/news/government/2023/08/21/new-federal-rules-college-mergers-cause-delays-concerns.

Kutner, Max. (2014). "How to Game the College Rankings." *Boston Magazine*, August 26, 2014. Accessed September 6, 2024. https://www.bostonmagazine.com/news/2014/08/26/how-northeastern-gamed-the-college-rankings/.

Lem, Stanislaw. (1968 [translation 1983]). *His Master's Voice*. New York: Harcourt Brace Jovanovich.

Levine, Phillip. (2022). *A Problem of Fit: How the Complexity of College Pricing Hurts Students—and Universities*. Chicago: University of Chicago Press.

Marcy, Mary B. (2023). "The 7 Trends Shaping Small Colleges." *Chronicle of Higher Education*, April 27, 2023. Accessed September 6, 2024. https://www.chronicle.com/article/the-7-trends-shaping-small-colleges.

Matthews, A. (1991). "Alma Maters Court Their Daughters." *New York Times Magazine*, April 7, 1991, p. 40 ff.

McBrayer, Justin P. (2022). "Diversity Statements Are the New Faith Statements." *Inside Higher Ed*, May 22, 2022. Accessed September 5, 2024. https://www.insidehighered.com/views/2022/05/23/diversity-statements-are-new-faith-statements-opinion.

McCraw, Thomas K. (2007). *Prophet of Innovation: Joseph Schumpeter and Creative Destruction*. Cambridge, MA: Belknap Press.

National Association of College and University Business Officers. (2024). "2024 NACUBO-Commonfund Study of Endowments." Accessed August 5, 2025. https://www.nacubo.org/Research/2024/NACUBO-Commonfund-Study-of-Endowments.

National Center for Education Statistics. (n.d.). "Maryville College Institutional Profile." Accessed September 5, 2024. https://nces.ed.gov/ipeds/institution-profile/220710.

Olson, Mancur. (1965). *The Logic of Collective Action: Public Goods and the Theory of Groups*. Cambridge, MA: Harvard University Press.

Palmer, Kathryn. (2024). "Dickinson State President Resigns, Blaming Nursing Board." *Inside Higher Ed*, July 16, 2024. Accessed September 6, 2024. https://www.insidehighered.com/news/governance/executive-leadership/2024/07/16/dickinson-state-president-resigns-blames-nursing.

Rhode, Deborah L. (2006). *In Pursuit of Knowledge: Scholars, Status, and Academic Culture*. Stanford, CA: Stanford University Press.

Rosenberg, John S. (2024). "Harvard Discloses Administrator and Investment Manager Compensation." *Harvard Magazine*, May 10, 2024. Accessed September 4, 2024. https://www.harvardmagazine.com/2024/05/top-harvard-salaries-announced.

Samek, Anya, and Chuck Longfield. (2023). "Do Thank-You Calls Increase Charitable Giving? Expert Forecasts and Field Experimental Evidence." *American Economic Journal: Applied Economics* 15(2):103–124.

Schelling, Thomas. (1978). *Micromotives and Macrobehavior*. New York: W. W. Norton.

Schultz, Robert, and Anna Stansbury. (2022). "Socioeconomic Diversity of Economics PhDs." Peterson Institute for International Economics Working Paper No. 22–4. Accessed September 5, 2024. https://papers.ssrn.com/sol3/papers.cfm?abstract_id=4068831.

Schwartz, Natalie. (2022). "Florida Passes Bill Pushing Accreditor Changes, Post-tenure Review." *Higher Ed Dive*, March 10, 2022. Accessed September 6, 2024. https://www.highereddive.com/news/florida-passes-bill-pushing-accreditor-changes-post-tenure-review/620220/.

Swensen, David F. (2000). *Pioneering Portfolio Management: An Unconventional Approach to Institutional Investment*. New York: Free Press.

Taleb, Nassim. (2007). *The Black Swan: The Impact of the Highly Improbable*. New York: Random House.

Tarrant, Melissa, Nathaniel Bray, and Stephen Katsinas. (2018). "The Invisible Colleges Revisited: An Empirical Review." *Journal of Higher Education* 89(3):341–367.

U.S. News & World Report. (2023). "U.S. News Announces Survey Distribution Date and Outcomes-Focused Updates to Methodology for Upcoming Best Colleges Rankings." Accessed September 6, 2024. https://www.usnews.com/info/blogs/press-room/articles/2023-05-19/u-s-news-announces-survey-distribution-date-and-outcomes-focused-updates-to-methodology-for-upcoming-best-colleges-rankings.

Veblen, Thorstein. (1899 [1953]). *The Theory of the Leisure Class*. New York: New American Library.

Veblen, Thorstein. (1918 [2015]). *The Higher Learning in America: A Memorandum on the Conduct of Universities by Business Men*. Baltimore, MD: Johns Hopkins University Press.

Wedgwood, C. V. (1959). *The King's War: 1641–1647* (v. 2 of The Great Rebellion). New York: MacMillan Company.

Weisbrod, Burton A. (1988). *The Nonprofit Economy*. Cambridge, MA: Harvard University Press.

Weitzman, Martin. (2007). "A Review of the *Stern Review on the Economics of Climate Change*." *Journal of Economic Literature* 45(3):703–724.

Wingfield, Mark. (2023). "Bob Jones University President Resigns in Battle with Board Chairman." *Baptist News Global*, March 31, 2023. Accessed September 5, 2024. https://baptistnews.com/article/bob-jones-university-president-resigns-in-battle-with-board-chairman/.

Zahneis, Megan. (2024). "After Sparking a Mass Resignation of Nursing Professors, This College President Resigned, Too." *Chronicle of Higher Education*, July 15, 2024. Accessed September 6, 2024. https://www.chronicle.com/article/after-sparking-a-mass-resignation-of-nursing-professors-this-college-president-resigned-too.

Index

About the Author

WILLIAM T. (TOM) BOGART is president emeritus of Maryville College. He also served as president of Columbia College in South Carolina, as dean of academic affairs at York College of Pennsylvania, and on the faculty of the Weatherhead School of Management at Case Western Reserve University. Dr. Bogart earned a PhD in economics from Princeton University and a BA in economics and mathematical sciences from Rice University. His previous books are *The Economics of Cities and Suburbs* and *Don't Call It Sprawl: Metropolitan Structure in the Twenty-First Century*. Tom lives in University Heights, Ohio, with his wife, Mary.